Ludington High School Library

CAREERS IN
HEALTH CARE

GENERAL EDITORS

Dale C. Garell, M.D.
Medical Director, California Children Services, Department of Health Services, County of Los Angeles
Clinical Professor, Department of Pediatrics & Family Medicine, University of Southern California School of Medicine
Former president, Society for Adolescent Medicine

Solomon H. Snyder, M.D.
Distinguished Service Professor of Neuroscience, Pharmacology, and Psychiatry, Johns Hopkins University School of Medicine
Former president, Society of Neuroscience
Albert Lasker Award in Medical Research, 1978

CONSULTING EDITORS

Robert W. Blum, M.D., Ph.D.
Associate Professor, School of Public Health and Department of Pediatrics
Director, Adolescent Health Program, University of Minnesota
Consultant, World Health Organization

Charles E. Irwin, Jr., M.D.
Associate Professor of Pediatrics
Director, Division of Adolescent Medicine, University of California, San Francisco

Lloyd J. Kolbe, Ph.D.
Chief, Office of School Health & Special Projects, Center for Health Promotion & Education, Centers for Disease Control
President, American School Health Association

Jordan J. Popkin
Director, Division of Federal Employee Occupational Health, U.S. Public Health Service Region I

Joseph L. Rauh, M.D.
Professor of Pediatrics and Medicine, Adolescent Medicine, Children's Hospital Medical Center, Cincinnati
Former president, Society for Adolescent Medicine

MEDICAL ISSUES

Dale C. Garell, M.D. • General Editor

CAREERS IN HEALTH CARE

Rachel Epstein

Introduction by C. Everett Koop, M.D., Sc.D.
Surgeon General, U.S. Public Health Service

CHELSEA HOUSE PUBLISHERS
New York • Philadelphia

The goal of the ENCYCLOPEDIA OF HEALTH is to provide general information in the ever-changing areas of physiology, psychology, and related medical issues. The titles in this series are not intended to take the place of the professional advice of a physician or other health-care professional.

Chelsea House Publishers
EDITOR-IN-CHIEF Nancy Toff
EXECUTIVE EDITOR Remmel T. Nunn
MANAGING EDITOR Karyn Gullen Browne
COPY CHIEF Juliann Barbato
PICTURE EDITOR Adrian G. Allen
ART DIRECTOR Maria Epes
MANUFACTURING MANAGER Gerald Levine

The Encyclopedia of Health
SENIOR EDITOR Sam Tanenhaus

Staff for CAREERS IN HEALTH CARE
ASSISTANT EDITOR Laura Dolce
DEPUTY COPY CHIEF Ellen Scordato
EDITORIAL ASSISTANT Jennifer Trachtenberg
PICTURE RESEARCHER Nisa Rauschenburg
DESIGNER Marjorie Zaum
PRODUCTION COORDINATOR Joseph Romano

Copyright © 1989 by Chelsea House Publishers, a division of Main Line Book Co. All rights reserved. Printed and bound in the United States of America.

First Printing

1 3 5 7 9 8 6 4 2

Library of Congress Cataloging-in-Publication Data

Epstein, Rachel S.
  Careers in health care / Rachel Epstein; introduction by C. Everett Koop.
    p. cm.—(The Encyclopedia of health. Medical issues)
  Bibliography: p.
  Includes index.
  ISBN 0-7910-0081-8. ISBN 0-7910-0518-6 (pbk.)
    1. Medical personnel—United States—Vocational guidance.
  I. Title. II. Series.
R690.E67 1989   88-30163
610.69'0973—dc19   CIP

CONTENTS

Prevention and Education:
The Keys to Good Health—
C. Everett Koop, M.D., Sc.D.   7

Foreword—Dale C. Garell, M.D.   9

Author's Preface   13

1 The Changing World of Health Care   17

2 Becoming a Practitioner   23

3 The Primary-Care Specialties   31

4 Surgical Specialties   39

5 Major Medical Specialties   47

6 Careers in Nursing   61

7 Dentistry   75

8 Allied Health Careers   87

9 Accepting the Challenge   95

Appendix: For More Information   97

Further Reading   99

Glossary   101

Index   104

THE ENCYCLOPEDIA OF HEALTH

THE HEALTHY BODY

The Circulatory System
Dental Health
The Digestive System
The Endocrine System
Exercise
Genetics & Heredity
The Human Body: An Overview
Hygiene
The Immune System
Memory & Learning
The Musculoskeletal System
The Neurological System
Nutrition
The Reproductive System
The Respiratory System
The Senses
Speech & Hearing
Sports Medicine
Vision
Vitamins & Minerals

THE LIFE CYCLE

Adolescence
Adulthood
Aging
Childhood
Death & Dying
The Family
Friendship & Love
Pregnancy & Birth

MEDICAL ISSUES

Careers in Health Care
Environmental Health
Folk Medicine
Health Care Delivery
Holistic Medicine
Medical Ethics
Medical Fakes & Frauds
Medical Technology
Medicine & the Law
Occupational Health
Public Health

PSYCHOLOGICAL DISORDERS AND THEIR TREATMENT

Anxiety & Phobias
Child Abuse
Compulsive Behavior
Delinquency & Criminal Behavior
Depression
Diagnosing & Treating Mental Illness
Eating Habits & Disorders
Learning Disabilities
Mental Retardation
Personality Disorders
Schizophrenia
Stress Management
Suicide

MEDICAL DISORDERS AND THEIR TREATMENT

AIDS
Allergies
Alzheimer's Disease
Arthritis
Birth Defects
Cancer
The Common Cold
Diabetes
Drugs: Prescription & OTC
First Aid & Emergency Medicine
Gynecological Disorders
Headaches
The Hospital
Kidney Disorders
Medical Diagnosis
The Mind-Body Connection
Mononucleosis & Other Infectious Diseases
Nuclear Medicine
Organ Transplants
Pain
Physical Handicaps
Poisons & Toxins
Sexually Transmitted Diseases
Skin Diseases
Stroke & Heart Disease
Substance Abuse
Tropical Medicine

PREVENTION AND EDUCATION: THE KEYS TO GOOD HEALTH

C. Everett Koop, M.D., Sc.D.
Surgeon General,
U.S. Public Health Service

The issue of health education has received particular attention in recent years because of the presence of AIDS in the news. But our response to this particular tragedy points up a number of broader issues that doctors, public health officials, educators, and the public face. In particular, it points up the necessity for sound health education for citizens of all ages.

Over the past 25 years this country has been able to bring about dramatic declines in the death rates for heart disease, stroke, accidents, and, for people under the age of 45, cancer. Today, Americans generally eat better and take better care of themselves than ever before. Thus, with the help of modern science and technology, they have a better chance of surviving serious—even catastrophic—illnesses. That's the good news.

But, like every phonograph record, there's a flip side, and one with special significance for young adults. According to a report issued in 1979 by Dr. Julius Richmond, my predecessor as Surgeon General, Americans aged 15 to 24 had a higher death rate in 1979 than they did 20 years earlier. The causes: violent death and injury, alcohol and drug abuse, unwanted pregnancies, and sexually transmitted diseases. Adolescents are particularly vulnerable, because they are beginning to explore their own sexuality and perhaps to experiment with drugs. The need for educating young people is critical, and the price of neglect is high.

Yet even for the population as a whole, our health is still far from what it could be. Why? A 1974 Canadian government report attributed all death and disease to four broad elements: inadequacies in the health-care system, behavioral factors or unhealthy life-styles, environmental hazards, and human biological factors.

To be sure, there are diseases that are still beyond the control of even our advanced medical knowledge and techniques. And despite yearnings that are as old as the human race itself, there is no "fountain of youth" to ward off aging and death. Still, there is a solution to many of the problems that undermine sound health. In a word, that solution is prevention. Prevention, which includes health promotion and education, saves lives, improves the quality of life, and, in the long run, saves money.

In the United States, organized public health activities and preventive medicine have a long history. Important milestones include the improvement of sanitary procedures and the development of pasteurized milk in the late 19th century, and the introduction in the mid-20th century of effective vaccines against polio, measles, German measles, mumps, and other once-rampant diseases. Internationally, organized public health efforts began on a wide-scale basis with the International Sanitary Conference of 1851, to which 12 nations sent representatives. The World Health Organization, founded in 1948, continues these efforts under the aegis of the United Nations, with particular emphasis on combatting communicable diseases and the training of health-care workers.

But despite these accomplishments, much remains to be done in the field of prevention. For too long, we have had a medical care system that is science- and technology-based, focused, essentially, on illness and mortality. It is now patently obvious that both the social and the economic costs of such a system are becoming insupportable.

Implementing prevention—and its corollaries, health education and promotion—is the job of several groups of people:

First, the medical and scientific professions need to continue basic scientific research, and here we are making considerable progress. But increased concern with prevention will also have a decided impact on how primary-care doctors practice medicine. With a shift to health-based rather than morbidity-based medicine, the role of the "new physician" will include a healthy dose of patient education.

Second, practitioners of the social and behavioral sciences—psychologists, economists, city planners—along with lawyers, business leaders, and government officials—must solve the practical and ethical dilemmas confronting us: poverty, crime, civil rights, literacy, education, employment, housing, sanitation, environmental protection, health care delivery systems, and so forth. All of these issues affect public health.

Introduction

Third is the public at large. We'll consider that very important group in a moment.

Fourth, and the linchpin in this effort, is the public health profession—doctors, epidemiologists, teachers—who must harness the professional expertise of the first two groups and the common sense and cooperation of the third, the public. They must define the problems statistically and qualitatively and then help us set priorities for finding the solutions.

To a very large extent, improving those statistics is the responsibility of every individual. So let's consider more specifically what the role of the individual should be and why health education is so important to that role. First, and most obviously, individuals can protect themselves from illness and injury and thus minimize their need for professional medical care. They can eat a nutritious diet, get adequate exercise, avoid tobacco, alcohol, and drugs, and take prudent steps to avoid accidents. The proverbial "apple a day keeps the doctor away" is not so far from the truth, after all.

Second, individuals should actively participate in their own medical care. They should schedule regular medical and dental checkups. Should they develop an illness or injury, they should know when to treat themselves and when to seek professional help. To gain the maximum benefit from any medical treatment that they do require, individuals must become partners in that treatment. For instance, they should understand the effects and side effects of medications. I counsel young physicians that there is no such thing as too much information when talking with patients. But the corollary is the patient must know enough about the nuts and bolts of the healing process to understand what the doctor is telling him. That is at least partially the patient's responsibility.

Education is equally necessary for us to understand the ethical and public policy issues in health care today. Sometimes individuals will encounter these issues in making decisions about their own treatment or that of family members. Other citizens may encounter them as jurors in medical malpractice cases. But we all become involved, indirectly, when we elect our public officials, from school board members to the president. Should surrogate parenting be legal? To what extent is drug testing desirable, legal, or necessary? Should there be public funding for family planning, hospitals, various types of medical research, and medical care for the indigent? How should we allocate scant technological resources, such as kidney dialysis and organ transplants? What is the proper role of government in protecting the rights of patients?

What are the broad goals of public health in the United States today? In 1980, the Public Health Service issued a report aptly entitled *Promoting Health-Preventing Disease: Objectives for the Nation.* This report expressed its goals in terms of mortality and in terms of intermediate goals in education and health improvement. It identified 15 major concerns: controlling high blood pressure; improving family planning; improving pregnancy care and infant health; increasing the rate of immunization; controlling sexually transmitted diseases; controlling the presence of toxic agents and radiation in the environment; improving occupational safety and health; preventing accidents; promoting water fluoridation and dental health; controlling infectious diseases; decreasing smoking; decreasing alcohol and drug abuse; improving nutrition; promoting physical fitness and exercise; and controlling stress and violent behavior.

For healthy adolescents and young adults (ages 15 to 24), the specific goal was a 20% reduction in deaths, with a special focus on motor vehicle injuries and alcohol and drug abuse. For adults (ages 25 to 64), the aim was 25% fewer deaths, with a concentration on heart attacks, strokes, and cancers.

Smoking is perhaps the best example of how individual behavior can have a direct impact on health. Today cigarette smoking is recognized as the most important single preventable cause of death in our society. It is responsible for more cancers and more cancer deaths than any other known agent; is a prime risk factor for heart and blood vessel disease, chronic bronchitis, and emphysema; and is a frequent cause of complications in pregnancies and of babies born prematurely, underweight, or with potentially fatal respiratory and cardiovascular problems.

Since the release of the Surgeon General's first report on smoking in 1964, the proportion of adult smokers has declined substantially, from 43% in 1965 to 30.5% in 1985. Since 1965, 37 million people have quit smoking. Although there is still much work to be done if we are to become a "smoke-free society," it is heartening to note that public health and public education efforts—such as warnings on cigarette packages and bans on broadcast advertising—have already had significant effects.

In 1835, Alexis de Tocqueville, a French visitor to America, wrote, "In America the passion for physical well-being is general." Today, as then, health and fitness are front-page items. But with the greater scientific and technological resources now available to us, we are in a far stronger position to make good health care available to everyone. And with the greater technological threats to us as we approach the 21st century, the need to do so is more urgent than ever before. Comprehensive information about basic biology, preventive medicine, medical and surgical treatments, and related ethical and public policy issues can help you arm yourself with the knowledge you need to be healthy throughout your life.

FOREWORD

Dale C. Garell, M.D.

Advances in our understanding of health and disease during the 20th century have been truly remarkable. Indeed, it could be argued that modern health care is one of the greatest accomplishments in all of human history. In the early 1900s, improvements in sanitation, water treatment, and sewage disposal reduced death rates and increased longevity. Previously untreatable illnesses can now be managed with antibiotics, immunizations, and modern surgical techniques. Discoveries in the fields of immunology, genetic diagnosis, and organ transplantation are revolutionizing the prevention and treatment of disease. Modern medicine is even making inroads against cancer and heart disease, two of the leading causes of death in the United States.

Although there is much to be proud of, medicine continues to face enormous challenges. Science has vanquished diseases such as smallpox and polio, but new killers, most notably AIDS, confront us. Moreover, we now victimize ourselves with what some have called "diseases of choice," or those brought on by drug and alcohol abuse, bad eating habits, and mismanagement of the stresses and strains of contemporary life. The very technology that is doing so much to prolong life has brought with it previously unimaginable ethical dilemmas related to issues of death and dying. The rising cost of health-care is a matter of central concern to us all. And violence in the form of automobile accidents, homicide, and suicide remain the major killers of young adults.

In the past, most people were content to leave health care and medical treatment in the hands of professionals. But since the 1960s, the consumer of medical care—that is, the patient—has assumed an increasingly central role in the management of his or her own health. There has also been a new emphasis placed on prevention: People are recognizing that their own actions can help prevent many of the conditions that have caused death and disease in the past. This accounts for the growing commitment to good nutrition and regular exercise, for the fact that more and more people are choosing not to smoke, and for a new moderation in people's drinking habits.

People want to know more about themselves and their own health. They are curious about their body: its anatomy, physiology, and biochemistry. They want to keep up with rapidly evolving medical technologies and procedures. They are willing to educate themselves about common disorders and diseases so that they can be full partners in their own health-care.

The ENCYCLOPEDIA OF HEALTH is designed to provide the basic knowledge that readers will need if they are to take significant responsibility for their own health. It is also meant to serve as a frame of reference for further study and exploration. The ENCYCLOPEDIA is divided into five subsections: The Healthy Body; The Life Cycle; Medical Disorders & Their Treatment; Psychological Disorders & Their Treatment; and Medical Issues. For each topic covered by the ENCYCLOPEDIA, we present the essential facts about the relevant biology; the symptoms, diagnosis, and treatment of common diseases and disorders; and ways in which you can prevent or reduce the severity of health problems when that is possible. The ENCYCLOPEDIA also projects what may lie ahead in the way of future treatment or prevention strategies.

The broad range of topics and issues covered in the ENCYCLOPEDIA reflects the fact that human health encompasses physical, psychological, social, environmental, and spiritual well-being. Just as the mind and the body are inextricably linked, so, too, is the individual an integral part of the wider world that comprises his or her family, society, and environment. To discuss health in its broadest aspect it is necessary to explore the many ways in which it is connected to such fields as law, social science, public policy, economics, and even religion. And so, the ENCYCLOPEDIA is meant to be a bridge between science, medical technology, the world at large, and you. I hope that it will inspire you to pursue in greater depth particular areas of interest, and that you will take advantage of the suggestions for further reading and the lists of resources and organizations that can provide additional information.

AUTHOR'S PREFACE
IS A CAREER IN HEALTH CARE FOR YOU?

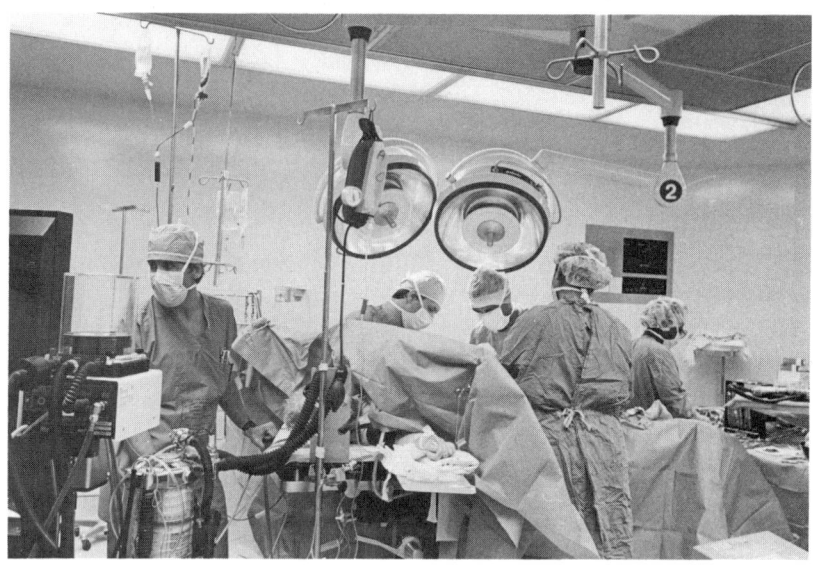

Are you intrigued by science? Are you challenged by the thought of putting it to work to help people? Are you stimulated by the prospect of daily involvement in life-and-death situations? If your answer to these questions is yes, then consider these: How will you cope with questions that have no answers or problems that cannot be solved? How will you react to seeing blood, broken bones, disfigurement, and other unpleasant sights common in the medical world? Will you be able to bear the knowledge that there are people whom you cannot save from fatal illness? And, more practically, are you a good student willing to attend an academic program for at least a year beyond high school and ready to spend untold hours studying?

If you are still able to answer yes to all these questions, then you should consider a career in health care. This field includes a wide array of professions. You can choose to become a surgeon who must make split-second decisions that are a matter of life and death. You can also perform research that requires years of laboratory work but may eventually save or improve thousands, even millions, of lives. In health care you can work with the elderly—who will make up an increasing percentage of the United States's population after the year 2000—or with premature infants who weigh as little as 2 pounds.

Within these areas—and they are only a few among hundreds—there are many different roles that need to be filled. Open-heart surgery, for example, demands not only the skills of the dexterous specialist responsible for precisely attaching microscopic blood vessels but also those of a scrub nurse, who helps the surgeon prepare for the operation and, during the delicate surgery, hands the doctor the instruments needed during the work. Other important tasks are performed by the anesthesiologist and the nurse anesthetist, who see to the patient's comfort, administer the correct anesthesia, and monitor the patient until the operation is over.

Health care also offers many options within a single career. Many doctors see patients, teach at a medical school, and conduct their own research. A nurse can work with children and also plan community health projects. A medical laboratory technologist may be employed either in a hospital laboratory or in the smaller setting of a doctor's office. No matter what particular health-care position you choose, you will provide a service to others and make a difference in their lives.

Careers in health care have their share of frustrations and disadvantages. For example, people employed in the field are aware of a very rigid hierarchy. In a typical hospital, physicians stand at the top level, followed by residents (doctors in training), and then by others whose status is often based on the amount

Author's Preface: Is a Career in Health Care for You?

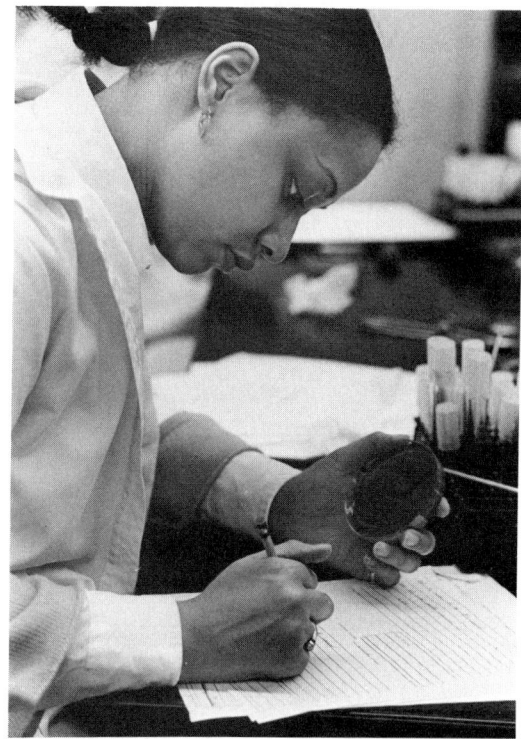

A technician records the contents of a petri dish. In addition to providing health care, contemporary hospitals conduct laboratory analysis and research.

of education required to do their job, such as X-ray technicians, nurses, and laboratory technicians. Those at the top of the ladder are the most highly paid and are accorded the most prestige. In addition, they are often granted more authority than they deserve. Thus, an experienced nurse may find his or her well-considered suggestions for patient care ignored by a resident barely out of medical school.

This volume outlines general trends in health care. It also reviews different careers in medicine, dentistry, nursing, and allied health-care areas. Some of the jobs it describes—such as those of a pediatrician and a school nurse—will be familiar to you. Others, such as those of perfusionists and midwives, may not be.

As you read about a job, picture yourself handling it. If a particular career appeals to you, try to find out more about it. The bibliography at the end of this book is a good place to begin. Next, speak with health-care professionals. There are many in every community, and they can lead you to specialists who can answer your specific questions.

To get hands-on experience in a health-care field, look for a part-time or summer job in a doctor's office or volunteer at your local hospital. There is no better way to see up close what professionals in this vast field do.

•   •   •   •

CHAPTER 1

THE CHANGING WORLD OF HEALTH CARE

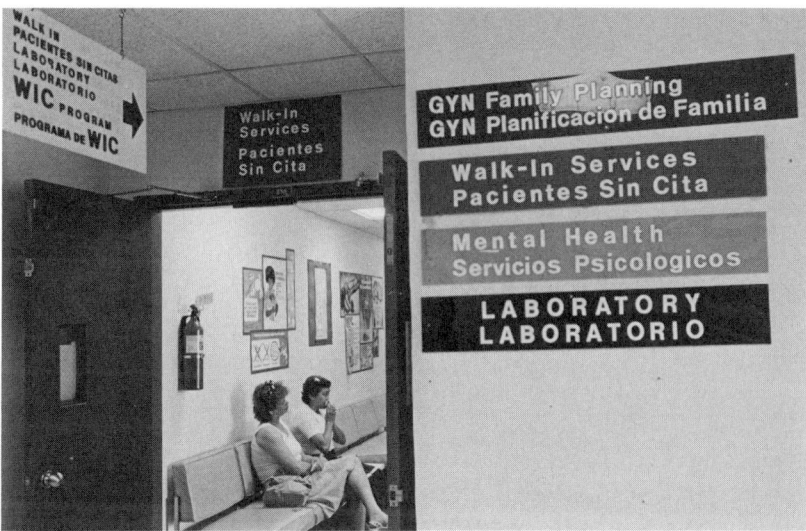

Much of America's economy is tied to health care. More than $1 of every $10 spent in this country—by individuals, corporations, and the government—goes toward improving our physical or mental well-being. And, like so many sectors of the economy, health care is rapidly changing.

High technology has added a new dimension to medicine as advanced research techniques enable us to discover new causes of and cures for diseases. This technology is altering the role of many physicians. Before long, a growing number will probably become superspecialists, concerned less with total patient care and more with scientific knowledge and with particular, even minute, areas of the body. As specialization grows, nurses and professionals in allied health careers will become more involved with the humane—or "people"—side of health care.

Another important change is the increased number of female physicians in the United States. In 1970, only 7.6% of physicians were women. By 1984, however, 34% of the students entering medical school were women. This growth is not expected to exceed 40%, the projected percentage for the class entering medical schools in the year 2000.

Today, the average patient is also sophisticated about health. In the past, patients passively accepted whatever their doctors told them. Now, however, the media inform the public of the newest developments in medicine, and patients demand this care from their doctors. Also, many health-insurance plans require a second opinion from a different doctor before approving expensive procedures such as surgery. This measure has helped turn patients into shrewd health-care consumers.

A parallel development is Americans' greater interest in fitness and wellness. This means that many people are not satisfied with being disease-free. They also want to feel as good as they possibly can. They are more likely to watch their diets—which means more work for nutritionists—and also to exercise, which can mean more work for orthopedic surgeons, who fix broken bones. These developments should also lead to less work for cardiologists and some oncologists (cancer specialists).

Regarding the traditional role of physician, according to the Bureau of Health Professions of the United States Department of Health and Human Services, there will be 643,000 physicians in practice in the year 2000—145,000 more than the forecasted requirement. This oversupply of physicians may mean that doctors, who have always been among the most highly paid members of our society, will see their incomes shrink. Physicians will be forced to compete with one another or with large corporate health-care plans. Doctors may hire marketing firms that will present physicians' services to the public as both necessary and attractive. On the advice of marketing firms, some physicians may specialize in fields in which there are few competitors.

The Changing World of Health Care

The number of women physicians has grown dramatically in recent years. In 1970, women composed only 7.6% of America's doctors; by 1984, they composed 34%.

The changing health-care economy affects not only those who work in the field but also those whom it serves. In the 1960s and 1970s, costs for health care climbed at a much higher rate than costs for most other services. Many Americans rebelled against what they interpreted to be the excessive expenses of hospitals and of physicians, especially those with fee-for-service practices—that is, practices that charge each patient for each visit.

In the United States, many people do not pay medical expenses out of their own pocket. Instead they are covered by medical insurance such as Blue Cross (which pays for hospital costs) and Blue Shield (which covers doctor's visits). Other plans include Medicaid, a federally financed, state-operated program of medical assistance to patients with low incomes, and Medicare, a federal program for people 65 or older. These programs either reimburse patients or make payments directly to doctors and hospitals.

Health-insurance companies mounted the first assault against skyrocketing medical costs. They did so by refusing to pay for certain procedures or to pay more than a fixed amount for approved procedures. The next step was the creation of diagnosis-related groups (DRGs), employing a coding system that specifies which procedures the insurer will cover. DRGs limit the payments for the number of days a patient can be hospitalized, the number of tests, and the cost of procedures. For example, if the DRG code for appendicitis specifies a three-day stay in the hospital and two blood tests, the hospital will be reimbursed for that exact cost. If a patient stays in the hospital an extra day, the hospital loses money. If he or she is discharged after two days, the hospital profits. DRGs usually exclude experimental or inordinately costly surgery, such as heart transplants. Since 1983, DRGs have been used not only by Medicare but also by a rising number of private insurance companies.

Another government-encouraged development to reduce health-care costs is the increased number of group medical practices, which can take many forms. Single-specialty groups offer in-depth care in one particular area of health care, such as obstetrics and gynecology. Others cover a broad spectrum of care, from pediatrics (child care) to geriatrics (care for the aging). Often these groups include nurses and allied health personnel as well as physicians.

The most popular form of group practice is the health maintenance organization (HMO). HMOs are groups of health-care consumers served by physicians, physician groups, and hospitals—all under contract to provide the full gamut of health-care services. HMOs prefer to hire generalists—family practitioners, internists, and pediatricians. These "gatekeepers" manage patients' cases and determine whether to approve the services of specialists, which may represent out-of-pocket expenses for the HMO.

HMOs have no fee-for-service arrangement. Payment is based instead on "capitation," a fixed annual fee paid for every patient enrolled in the plan. The institution that has put together the HMO—often an employer, an insurance company, or group of investors—pays the fee to the doctors and hospital. If the patient is hospitalized for a long period of time or needs many diagnostic or treatment procedures, the HMO or hospital must absorb the extra cost, which whittles down their income. On the other hand, if expenses are lower than the initial fee, the hospital may profit and HMO doctors may earn an end-of-year bonus.

Doctors, patients, and health-care economists all differ widely about the value of HMOs. HMOs have acted, generally, to reduce the use of health resources. For example, in fee-for-service insurance plans, hospitalization rates fall between 700 and 1,100 hospitalizations per 1,000 enrollees (these figures take into account patients hospitalized more than once); with prepaid plans, such as HMOs, the rate drops to about 400 hospitalizations per 1,000 enrollees. At the same time, however, the reduction in hospital admissions means that those people who are hospitalized are often extremely sick and need intensive and very expensive care.

According to Dr. Alvin R. Tarlov, chairman of the 1980 Graduate Medical Education National Advisory Committee, HMOs and similar plans will cover 30% of the population by the year 1995. Given the physician-to-patient ratio of 120 doctors to each 100,000 people enrolled in HMOs compared with a ratio of more than 200 doctors to 100,000 patients in the fee-for-service sector, the spread of HMOs decreases the demand for doctors. By 1983, 39% of all physicians under 36 years of age had chosen to work for HMOs, group practices, clinics, or emergency rooms. In contrast, only 23% of those aged 36 to 45 preferred to join group practices.

For doctors, HMOs raise sticky problems. Dr. David Nash,

Group practices generally reduce the number of hospital visits made by subscribers, although emergency patients, such as this victim of a motorcycle accident, still depend on hospital services.

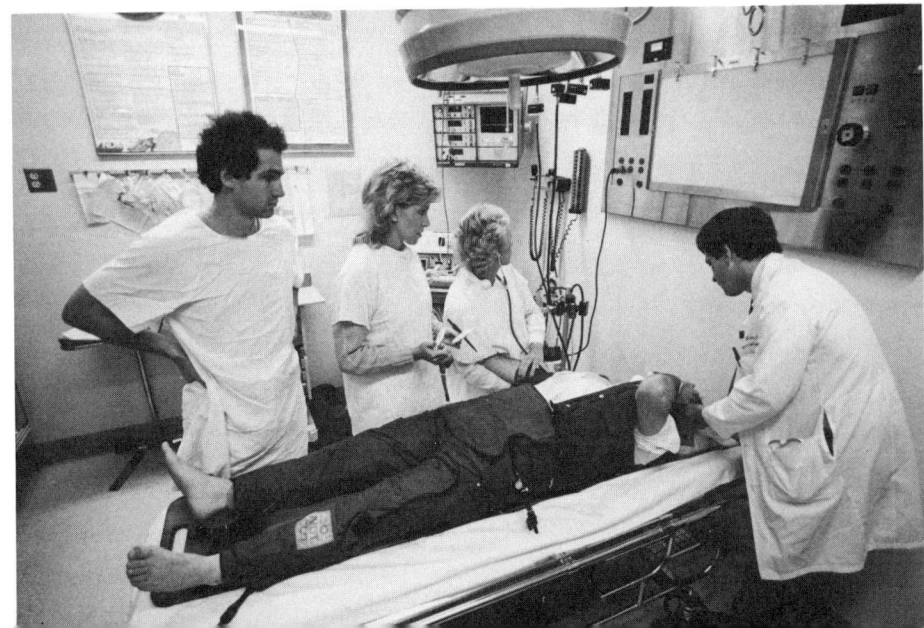

author of *Future Practice Alternatives in Medicine,* calls practice in an HMO "life in a fishbowl." "Good" practitioners qualify for bonuses if they do not use too many resources, order too many tests, or keep patients in the hospital for extended periods of time. Other doctors resent being put on the defensive by detailed questions from peers about why they recommended costly services.

There are also distinct advantages to working for an HMO. Many are economic, especially for young physicians daunted by the expense of malpractice insurance and by the cost of renting and staffing the office needed for private practice. Moreover, most young doctors have large education loans to repay and cannot afford the luxury of building up a full practice of private patients. HMOs thus offer an attractive alternative. They cover malpractice insurance premiums, provide an office and staff, and supply the new physician with a steady stream of patients. Doctors employed by HMOs work fewer hours and enjoy a more regular schedule than private practitioners, though they earn less money.

HMOs are not the only form of joint venture for physicians. Doctors who have built up fee-for-service practices sometimes join independent practice associations (IPAs) or preferred provider organizations (PPOs). These arrangements enable them to maintain their private practice and contract to provide services to HMO patients at a discount from their private-practice fees.

Through new developments in health care, such as HMOs, PPOs, and IPAs, the roles a health-care professional must take on are subtly changing. Now, more than ever, there is a great need to understand the direction in which health care is moving and adjust the educational trend to meet that demand. Young people deciding on a career in health care today have many more options to choose from and, consequently, a more difficult decision to make. When reading about different careers, keep in mind the new directions health care is branching off in and, if possible, choose a career not only best suited to your personality but also likely to remain a vital part of the changing world of health care.

• • • •

CHAPTER 2

BECOMING A PRACTITIONER

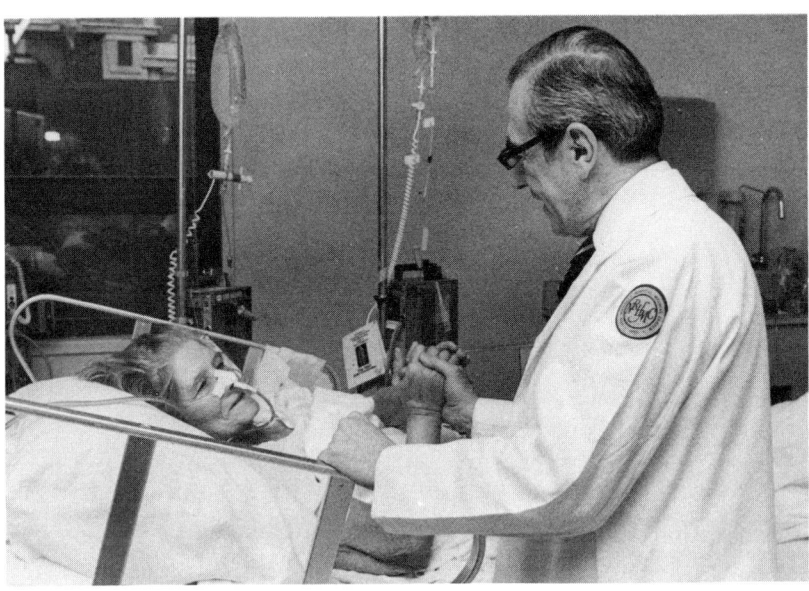

Becoming a physician involves long, hard work. Some people lay plans early, even in high school, when they augment the usual course load—English, a foreign language, history, math, and biology—with classes in chemistry and physics. Students can bolster their records—and test their interest in medicine—by working part-time in a hospital or other health-care setting. These activities may help the applicant get into a college with a premedical advising program and a good history of placing its students in medical school.

Once in college, students invariably face stiff competition from other premeds, all vying for the limited number of openings in the nation's 126 fully accredited medical schools. The vast majority of premeds major in biology, chemistry, or both. Those who choose other fields must still take a heavy load of science courses. Otherwise, they must add an extra year of course work after they graduate from college and before they apply to medical school.

It is not enough to pass these tough courses. One must excel. The mean grade-point average of all students admitted to first-year medical classes in 1987–88 was 3.45 (out of a possible 4.0). In addition, applicants to medical school must take the Medical College Admissions Test (MCAT), a seven-hour exam that includes sections on biology, chemistry, and physics. It also tests one's reading and analytic skills. The highest possible score for each section is 15; the average score is about 9. In the future, an essay may also be required. The applicant's MCAT results are weighed heavily by medical schools because the exam provides a more neutral basis of comparison than grade-point averages, which tend to fluctuate from college to college.

Medical school is costly. In the 1980s, tuitions ranged from more than $10,000 a year for residents at state schools to twice that amount for private schools. Roughly 68% of all medical students receive financial aid, more often in the form of loans than in the form of scholarships. In 1985, the average debt of a fourth-year medical school student was $30,256.

Of the America's 126 medical programs, 102 last 4 years. The other 24 offer a combined college and medical school program that takes 6 years and reduces the years of university-level study by 2 years. In the standard four-year program, students spend the first two years learning anatomy, biochemistry, physiology, pharmacology, microbiology, and pathology.

This course of study has increasingly come under fire. The 1984 report of the Association of American Medical Colleges, for example, urged faculties to place more emphasis on the humanitarian side of medicine. In response, a growing number of medical schools have revised their approach. Many have widened their curriculum to include training in ethics, genetic counseling,

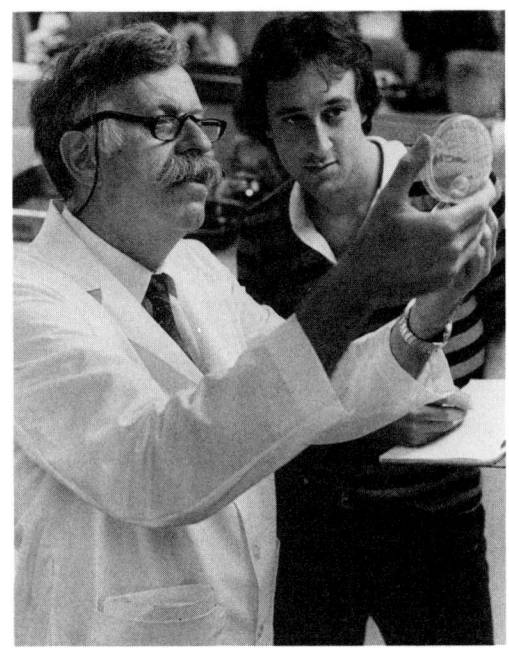

A histologist examines a tissue culture while a student looks on. In recent years, medical school faculty have begun to work more closely with individual students.

human sexuality, human values in medicine, patient education, and drug counseling.

Other programs have developed innovative approaches that depart from the curriculum just described. Perhaps the most widely known is the New Pathway program at Harvard Medical School, which replaces large lecture courses with small seminars. Each has only six to eight students who, led by a professor, discuss possible diagnoses and treatments by studying written cases of actual patients. In addition to considering physiological and biological symptoms, the students take into account issues such as the patient's career, family, and psychology. Students in this and similar programs now become involved with patient care as early as the first few weeks of medical school. This change in curriculum is designed to make physicians more sensitive to the human aspects of their work.

All programs—traditional or innovative—emphasize hands-on training in the students' third and fourth years, when they leave the classroom and gain their first experience in patient care—always in a supervised setting. The average student participates in eight clerkships, called *rotations*, that last approximately six weeks each and include the fields of internal medicine, obstetrics/gynecology, pediatrics, psychiatry, and surgery.

In their third and fourth years, medical students leave the classroom and the lab and, supervised by physicians, work directly with patients. Here neurosurgery interns observe as a doctor examines a patient.

Rotations teach students how to apply science to real-life situations and remind them that compassion is an essential component of health care. It may seem that young doctors naturally sympathize with the ill and the suffering—why else enter the profession? It is not so simple. The intense competition of the premed and medical school grind often hardens the outlook of fledgling physicians. And this hardness is reinforced when they first taste clinical experience under the supervision of resident physicians who may have become jaded by the burden of treating thousands of patients.

Most students recover their initial enthusiasm, however. They soon realize how important their services are, and their desire to attain a high level of professionalism drives them to perform the best possible job. And although the apprentice doctor may be taken aback by testy patients—who are usually uncomfortable, ill, and afraid—occasionally one patient will assert his or her individuality and humanity and help the student regain the compassion that guided him or her toward medicine in the first place.

What exactly do third- and fourth-year students do? Primarily, they work closely with residents, who have them take patient histories, administer blood tests and X rays, and examine patients. They take notes as they perform this last task and then show them to the resident, who comments on them and compares his or her own findings. Conscientious residents will usually consult with their students during the important stages of diagnosis and treatment. Students also assist in making rounds, that is, they visit all the patients under the care of a particular physician or in a particular specialty area and then bring the staff up-to-date on tests that have been run, the patients' current condition, and the dates when they are expected to be released from care.

Fourth-year medical school students apply for two- or three-year postgraduate, or residency, training programs in a hospital. There are a sufficient number of residency positions to accommodate virtually every medical school graduate. Still, there is intense competition for programs that offer the most interesting and varied patient care and the best staff of teachers and researchers. Different hospitals excel in different specialties, and some specialties can only be studied in certain hospitals.

Because the array of hospitals is so wide and the number of qualified applicants so high, the National Resident Matching Program in Evanston, Illinois matches up potential residents and programs. The program calls for students and hospitals to rank each other in order of preference. A computer compiles the results, and each student is then informed of his or her choice of hospitals. Spouses who both apply for residencies may end up in different hospitals in the same city.

In 1988 residents were paid salaries that averaged in the low $20,000s. They spend three-quarters of their time actively diagnosing and treating patients under the close supervision of the hospitals' staff physicians. Residents often complain of long hours, hard work, and not enough time to get to know the patients. Like medical students, residents are "on call" every fourth night, which means that for a designated stretch of time they work from 7:30 in the morning one day until 5:30 the following afternoon.

Before doctors can open their own practice, they must be licensed. In some states licenses are issued by the Department of Education; in others, by the Department of Health. The requirements for licensing include the following:

CAREERS IN HEALTH CARE

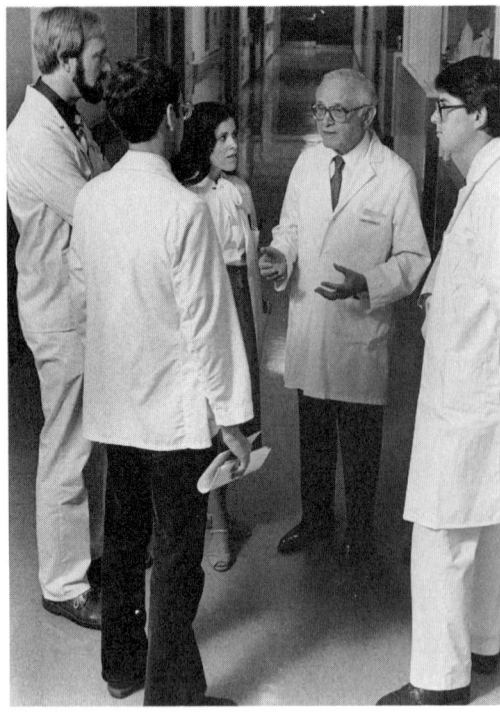

Advanced medical students accompany resident physicians on their daily rounds. Here a senior resident at a Boston hospital confers with students in between visits to patients.

1. Evidence of satisfactory completion of medical education at a school acceptable to the licensing authority.

2. One or two years (two to three years for graduates of foreign medical schools) of additional training after graduation from medical school (the residency period).

3. Evidence of good moral character, usually furnished by letters of reference from medical school teachers and personal friends.

4. Completion of an examination acceptable to the licensing authority. There are two examinations. About 75% of aspiring physicians take the exam that leads to certification by the National Board of Medical Examiners (NBME), an independent organization that tests graduates of U.S. and Canadian medical schools. The exam is divided into three parts. Students take the first part after their second year in medical school, the second after completing medical school, and the third during the first year of their residency.

The NBME exam is not recognized, however, in Texas, Louisiana, and the Virgin Islands. In those areas, doctors must pass the Federation Licensing Exam (FLEX), which is designed and scored by the Federation of State Medical Boards and administered by the individual states. The FLEX is taken in one sitting and only upon graduation from medical school.

In the United States, any doctor associated with a hospital, either as a staff member or as an attending physician, must submit to periodic reviews of his or her competency. The review process is supervised by the Joint Commission on Accreditation of Health Care Organizations, a national, voluntary agency made up of hospitals and doctors that sets standards for physicians and hospitals. One standard is that each patient must be attended daily by his or her physician. Another is that each hospital must ensure that each health-care practitioner provides only those services in which he or she is competent.

Every three years, each hospital in America is audited by a team of Joint Commission examiners. The hospital presents its most important records, such as minutes of meetings in which the doctors in each clinical department—surgery, internal medicine, neurology, and so on—evaluated their colleagues. The hospital's own peer review committee meets regularly to discuss a certain number of cases per doctor, without mentioning by name the doctor whose work is under review. Some cases are chosen at random for review; others, such as a mortality (death) case, always come under review.

During these conferences doctors run through a series of questions that aim to determine if any part of the case is questionable and if something different should have been done. The evaluating doctors understand that not every case ends happily, and that no matter what actions are taken by the physician, some patients will die. Nonetheless, the overall purpose of the sessions is to weed out the very few doctors whose actions fall below acceptable standards.

Yet another set of regulations is imposed on doctors by the Department of Health of their state, which requires that certain classes of incidents be discussed and reported. For example, any time a patient makes an unscheduled return to the operating room, this fact is noted on the doctor's record, as are complaints voiced by patients. If a doctor's dossier thickens with reported incidents, he or she may be investigated.

When doctors find that a physician has fallen below their standards, they can act in one of several ways. They can supervise the physician the next time he or she handles a similar procedure; recommend that the physician receive more training; revoke his or her authority to perform the procedure within the hospital (in New York State, each such reduction of a doctor's privileges must be reported to the state regulatory body); and finally—if the misconduct is life threatening—the doctor may be suspended from practice at the hospital. This last penalty is seldom used.

Most states require that all health-care providers be regularly reviewed to ensure that their performance matches their job description. Every two years doctors must be reappointed, subject to a review of their competency in a number of areas such as infection control, safety, blood transfusion, continuing medical education, complaints, and incident reports.

The purpose of these reviews is not merely to punish but also to offer help. If a doctor has a problem with drugs or alcohol or suffers a psychological imbalance, treatment is available through the physician impairment programs run by individual state and county medical societies. Initiated either at the physician's own request or on referral from a hospital peer review process, these confidential programs guarantee the public that physicians will continue or return to medical practice only when they are fully equipped to do so.

• • • •

CHAPTER 3

THE PRIMARY-CARE SPECIALTIES

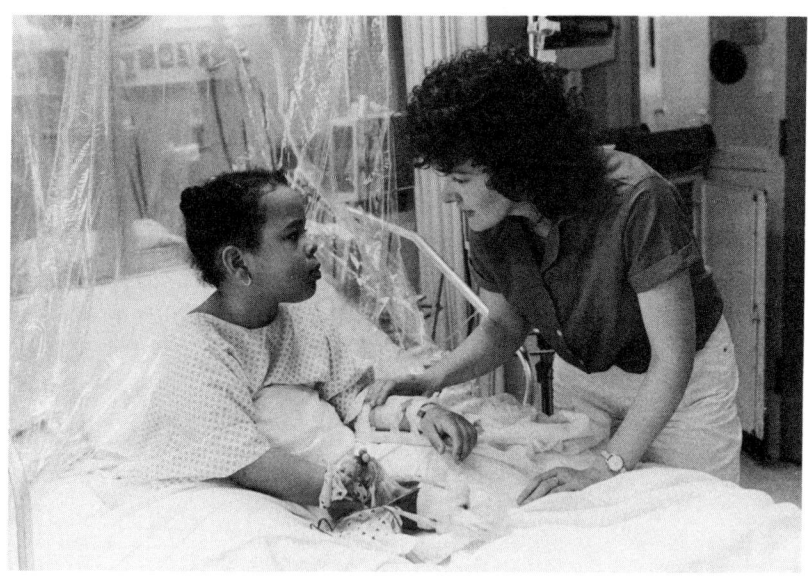

The middle decades of the 20th century saw an explosion of knowledge and technology relating to the human body. The wealth of information is so great that no single doctor can possibly keep up. As a result, the medical profession abounds in specialists who are educated in and keep up-to-date on the treatment of highly specific health problems.

Not all doctors pursue narrow specialties, however. There are also primary-care physicians, the men and women whom patients usually visit first when they do not feel well and need to know exactly what is wrong. Primary care includes the large specialties of internal medicine, pediatrics, and obstetrics and gynecology, along with the subspecialties of adolescent medicine and geriatrics. All these doctors deal with more than one aspect of a patient's health.

INTERNAL MEDICINE

Internal medicine, which is practiced by more than one physician in five, is the largest medical specialty and also one of the most general. Doctors of internal medicine provide overall health care and specialize in nonsurgical, or medical, treatment of the internal organs and functions of the body.

After medical school, internists enter a three-year residency program during which they are trained in the following areas: allergy and immunology (the study of tissue reactions to foreign substances); cardiology; hematology (the study of blood); oncology (the study of tumors); endocrinology (the study of hormones); infectious diseases; gastroenterology (the study of the digestive system); nephrology (the study of the kidneys); gerontology (the study of aging and the diseases of the elderly); pulmonary problems (lungs); and rheumatology (the study of connective tissues).

Patients visit internists for regular checkups and for the relief of minor discomforts such as headaches, sore throats, and muscle aches. They may also come with chronic problems requiring continuing care such as diabetes (a disorder caused by the failure of the pancreas to release enough insulin into the body). Internists are the detectives of medicine. First, they take a history that includes questions about the current and past health of the patient and his or her family. They then perform a variety of diagnostic tests, which often include basic blood tests and bacteriological cultures, such as those for strep throat. They may also do a urine analysis, a chest X-ray, or an electrocardiogram, which detects abnormal electrical impulses in the heart. When more technologically advanced and sophisticated tests are needed, experts perform them. It is the internist, however, who tells the expert what test to run and consults with him or her on the diagnosis.

The Primary-Care Specialties

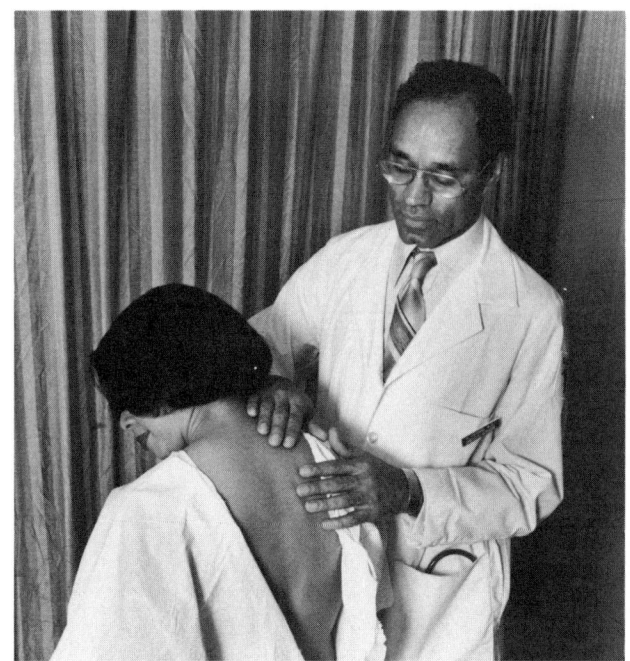

A crucial task performed by primary-care specialists is the preliminary examination. Here, a doctor at Harlem Hospital Medical Center, in New York City, checks a patient for early signs of cancer.

FAMILY MEDICINE

Doctors with family practices provide care to entire families from birth through old age. The philosophy of family medicine is that the whole patient should be taken into account and that family, social, and work relationships matter as much as the condition of specific organs. According to a November 1984 article in *The New Physician*, the family practitioner typically "receives the greatest satisfaction from intense involvement in the changing lives of patients, rather than from the treatment of the health problems they present."

During their three-year residency, family physicians learn to care for patients in an outpatient setting (during regular office visits) instead of a hospital. Their training includes obstetrics/gynecology, internal medicine, general surgery, pediatrics, geriatrics, psychiatry, community medicine, emergency medicine, orthopedics, ophthalmology, otolaryngology (ear, nose, and throat), urology, radiology, and practice management.

The doctor in training can handle so many areas because he

or she focuses on the most common diagnoses rather than on the esoteric or unusual occurrences that form the basis of other specialty training. If family practitioners encounter a situation they cannot diagnose, they consult other specialists. Nevertheless, family physicians manage 90% of the situations they encounter themselves, from delivering babies to correcting hernias to treating childhood infections.

In these days of cost-effective medical care, family physicians are in great demand, particularly by HMOs. As the supply of doctors grows relative to the population in the beginning of the 21st century, family physicians will be among the few specialists who will be in short supply.

PEDIATRICS

Pediatricians specialize in the care of children. They also must work closely with parents. Indeed, because most people know little about child care until they have a baby, much of the pediatrician's time is spent in teaching first-time parents the basics of daily baby care, such as how and when to give a bath and a shampoo, how to make the home safe, and how to take a baby's temperature. During the first few months of a baby's life, the pediatrician and a new mother may be in what seems like constant contact. For this reason, the pediatrician is often the first doctor called when the family has a medical problem, even if it does not involve the baby.

Pediatricians see babies for regular checkups according to the American Academy of Pediatrics, as often as 13 times during the child's first 2 years of life. After the child reaches the age of four, the visits taper down to once a year. These checkups can make up 60% of a pediatrician's practice.

The purpose of the checkups is to immunize the child against disease and to test for blood type and tuberculosis. During these visits, the doctor also makes sure the child is growing socially, mentally, and physically according to well-established norms for different ages. The pediatrician will also be called upon to answer many routine questions posed by parents.

The most common diagnosis made in a pediatrician's office is *otitis media*, the Latin name for middle-ear infection. Other common problems are allergies, appendicitis, warts, diaper rash, hernia (protrusion of an organ or part through the wall of a body cavity), teething, lice, measles, mumps, and chicken pox.

Pediatricians are trained in a three-year hospital residency begun after medical school. Some receive special training in areas such as pediatric cardiology, pediatric oncology, or pediatric surgery. There are also prenatal specialists, who treat babies whose problems are diagnosed before they are born, and neonatologists, who treat babies in the first 28 days of life.

OBSTETRICS AND GYNECOLOGY

Obstetricians deal with pregnant women; gynecologists deal with women's reproductive organs. They are two separate medical specialties, but they are usually combined in one medical practice. Often a doctor will concentrate more on obstetrics at the beginning of a career and then move on to gynecology as both the physician and the patients grow older. Also, the high cost of malpractice insurance for obstetricians is causing many physicians in this area to specialize in gynecology. An obstetrician/gynecologist treats patients both medically and surgically.

The obstetrician/gynecologist may be a woman's primary physician from the time she becomes sexually active through menopause, which signals the end of a woman's reproductive cycle. During this time, the patient visits the doctor once a year for an

An obstetrician visits a mother and her newborn child. Doctors usually combine a practice in obstetrics (treating pregnant women) with one in gynecology (treating diseases of the female reproductive system).

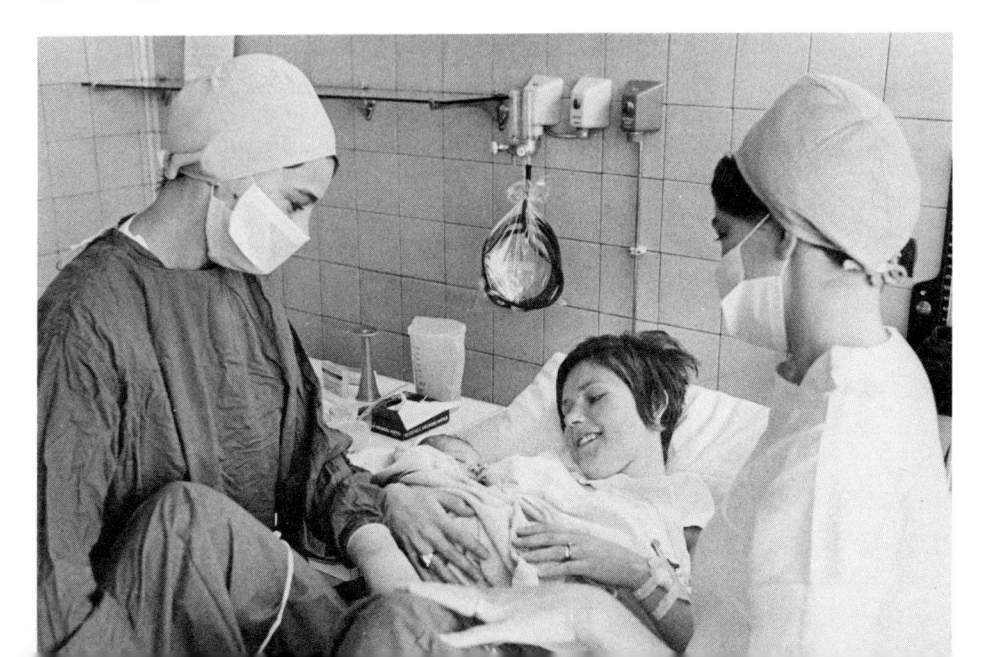

examination and a Pap test. This exam involves microscopic analysis of vaginal cells and is crucial in detecting and treating cervical cancer. Doctors often choose this particular medical specialty because it affords them long-term relationships with patients who are not always ill.

Gynecologists specialize in diseases of the vagina, uterus, cervix, fallopian tubes, ovaries, and breasts. Some of these are cancer, sexually transmitted diseases (STDs), and infections. Gynecologists may also deal with contraception (birth control), abortion (termination of a pregnancy), and infertility (a couple's inability to conceive a child).

Obstetricians treat pregnant women, advising them on nutrition, exercise, and smoking. They also monitor labor and deliver the baby, either vaginally, through the birth canal, or through abdominal surgery, known as a cesarean section. The obstetrician then cares for the mother and may even recommend a pediatrician.

Obstetricians/gynecologists also play a role in public health. Prominent members of the field advise government agencies on programs dealing with maternal health and mount campaigns for yearly Pap tests, safe birth control, and frequent doctor's visits during pregnancy.

ADOLESCENT MEDICINE

Adolescent medicine is recognized by the American Medical Association (AMA) as a subspecialty that does not require a certifying examination. Most practitioners of adolescent medicine are pediatricians, although some are internists and family practitioners. All have completed a one- or two-year fellowship in adolescent medicine.

Adolescents, technically defined as people between the ages of 13 and 22 years old, are in the process of growing from childhood into adulthood. This process includes physical changes—increased height and weight and development of secondary sex characteristics, such as the growth of body hair. It also includes psychological changes, as the child evolves an identity independent of the family; psychosexual changes, as an individual advances from sexually inactive childhood to sexually active adulthood; and cognitive changes, as one changes from a child who sees the world in concrete terms to an adult who can deal

The Primary-Care Specialties

with ambiguity and such abstract issues as time and the future.

Practitioners of adolescent medicine observe and encourage all these changes and also deal with the special problems of adolescence. These may include scoliosis, or curvature of the spine; acne; and psychological distress caused by dissatisfaction with a rapidly changing appearance. Specialists in adolescent medicine may also deal with sports injuries and with diseases, such as diabetes, whose effect on adolescents differs from its effect on adults.

According to Dr. S. Kenneth Schonberg, who in 1988 was President of the Society for Adolescent Medicine, "What is particularly fascinating about adolescent medicine is the relationship between behavior and health. This is true because accidents, homicide, and suicide are the leading causes of adolescent death, and pregnancy is the most common treatable health condition, and all of these relate to behavior over which the adolescent has some control."

There are 40 million adolescents in the United States, and only a few hundred practitioners of adolescent medicine. For that reason, practitioners of adolescent medicine consider one of their major tasks to be educating other doctors—notably pediatricians and internists—on the particular problems of adolescents, including the need for confidentiality.

GERIATRIC MEDICINE

Geriatrics is the branch of medicine that deals with aging and with the diagnosis and treatment of diseases affecting the elderly. Although a small subspecialty, it will probably grow significantly

As a growing number of Americans survive into old age, geriatrics will blossom into a major specialty that will require the services of nurses, who can often provide more personal care than doctors can.

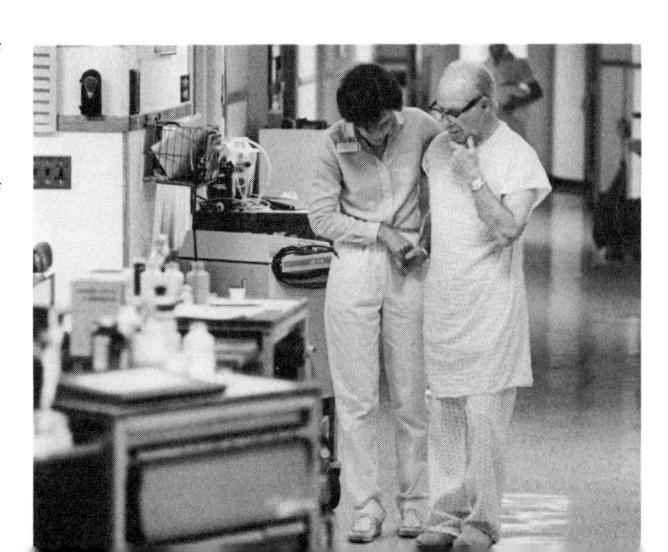

in the 21st century as America's population includes a greater proportion of people over the age of 65.

Geriatricians first receive training in internal medicine and then receive subspecialty training in geriatrics. They are involved not only with healthy elderly people but also with those who suffer from acute illnesses, with the chronically ill who can continue to look after themselves, and with those who must be institutionalized.

With patients in their sixties, physicians take every possible action to rid the body of disease, assuming that once the disease is cured health will be restored. Many elderly patients, however, have more than one physical or mental problem, and curing one problem often aggravates another and may still leave the patient unwell. Recognizing that the goals of treatment for older patients may be different than those of treatment for younger ones, geriatric medicine aims to

1. Maximize the patient's independence.
2. Ensure the patient's maximum comfort by alleviating physical discomfort and psychological stress.
3. Promote a sense of well-being.
4. Prevent premature death.
5. Minimize the cost of care without compromising its outcome.

Experts in geriatric medicine often serve as advocates for individual patients, explaining to families and institutions what must be done to ensure proper care. More publicly, these doctors speak up for older people as overlooked members of society with much to contribute to the world around them.

• • • •

CHAPTER 4

SURGICAL SPECIALTIES

Surgical procedures can be routine, 45-minute operations performed under a local anesthetic, wherein the patient is not put to sleep but has a limited area of his or her body made insensitive to pain. Operations can also be highly complex and lengthy. Abdominal surgery, for example, can last up to 14 hours, and during this time the diseased parts of the patient are resectioned and reconnected.

CAREERS IN HEALTH CARE

Surgeons often begin to specialize in their first postgraduate year and usually complete at least a four-year residency. For several decades, mainly as the result of dramatic breakthroughs in neurosurgery and open-heart surgery, surgeons have been the most glamorous members of the medical profession, highly paid and publicly lauded. But the growth of HMOs and other developments in cost containment may reduce opportunities for surgical subspecialists in the years to come.

SURGERY

Surgeons treat patients by cutting and removing diseased organs or tissue from the patient's body. This is in direct contrast to medical therapy, which treats diseases with chemical preparations. There is little analysis involved in the surgeon's job. In general, once the operation is finished, the results—whether favorable or not—are usually immediately clear.

The most common problems dealt with by surgeons include appendicitis, hernia, cancerous tumors of the breast and large intestine, and gall-bladder disease. Surgeons also remove growths from the skin and perform biopsies, the removal of tissue for examination before more surgery is performed. The surgeon not only performs operations but also talks with patients before surgery and in follow-up visits to the hospital after the procedure has been completed.

Surgeons need exceptional manual dexterity and cool heads; many split-second decisions must be made under extreme pressure. When operating on the heart or brain, any cessation of function can be fatal, and these delicate organs can fail at any time. And even in more routine operations, excessive blood loss must be dealt with immediately so that the patient does not bleed to death. Of course, there is always the possibility that something unexpected will occur on the operating table.

Surgeons must complete a residency that can be three to five years long, depending on the surgery subspecialty for which the resident is being trained. Among the important subspecialties are thoracic surgery (operations on heart and lungs); plastic surgery (repairs and corrections of missing, injured, or defective body parts); neurological surgery (operations on the nerve network, including the brain); and colon and rectal surgery.

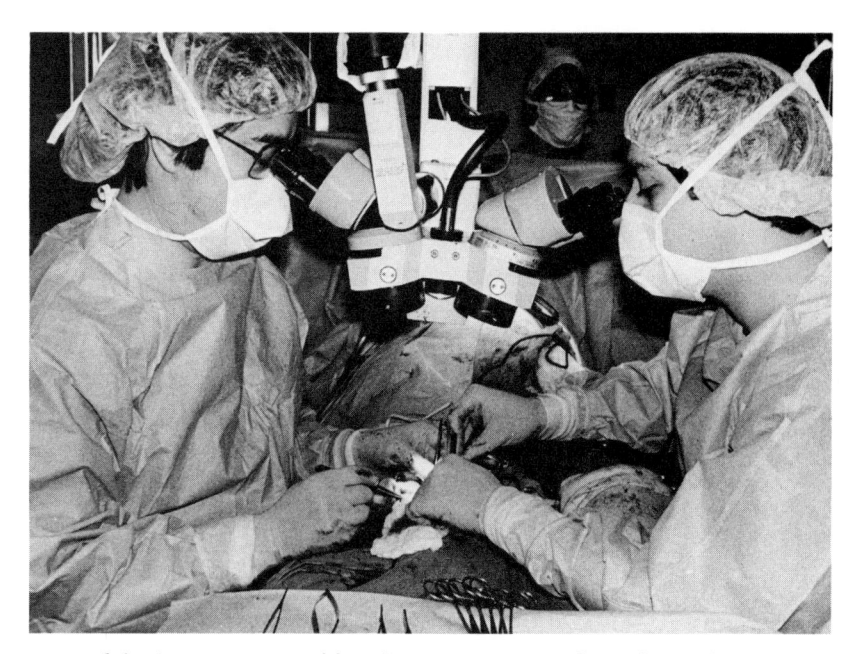

Powerful microscopes enable microsurgeons, such as those shown here, to perform delicate operations that not only cure patients but also spare them long periods of recuperation.

New progress has been made in surgery on the heart and blood vessels and in transplants of various organs, notably kidneys. Advances have also been made in microsurgery that enable surgeons to repair knee ligaments in a short procedure requiring almost no recuperation time and to reattach severed hands so that they may regain some ability to function. Surgeons also employ a number of new techniques. The most important of these is probably laser surgery. Lasers (the word is an acronym for light amplification by stimulated emission of radiation) produce a concentrated beam of pure light that can destroy diseased cells simply by being aimed at them. The high precision of laser surgery is especially useful on the nose, ears, mouth, throat, vagina, and other small, enclosed areas.

OPHTHALMOLOGY AND EYE CARE

Many health-care careers deal with eyes. The medical specialty of eye care is called ophthalmology. An ophthalmologist examines eyes for visual and medical problems, prescribes corrective lenses and medication, and, when necessary, performs surgery.

CAREERS IN HEALTH CARE

An eye examination includes tests for color, depth, and side (peripheral) perception. Eye examinations also disclose diseases, not only of the eye but also of the brain. The most common ophthalmological surgery is removal of cataracts, gray-white films that can form on the lens of the eye, limiting vision. Cataracts often occur in older people. Recently, surgeons have begun to remove cataracts on an outpatient basis, which means the patient does not stay overnight in the hospital. Other eye surgery includes raising droopy eyelids and correcting diseases of the cornea, the transparent front part of the eye.

Ophthalmologists must have good eye-hand coordination, depth perception, and color vision. They are trained in a four-year residency program after medical school. They can then go on to subspecialize in children's eye problems, corneal diseases, glaucoma (abnormally high pressure in the eye), plastic surgery, or low vision.

ORTHOPEDIC SURGERY

Orthopedic surgery deals with problems affecting the body's muscles and bones. Orthopedists treat backs, necks, arms, hands, legs, and feet. They also deal with injuries, which constitute one-

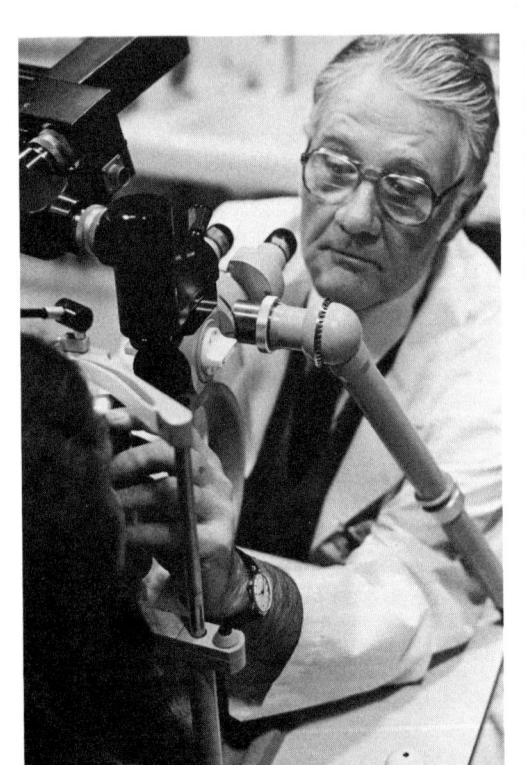

Like many other medical specialists, ophthalmologists rely on sophisticated technology. The apparatus shown here enables the doctor to examine the patient's retina and to test for glaucoma.

third of a typical orthopedic practice. Other common problems include arthritis and, to a lesser extent, tumors and infections of the bone and bone marrow. Orthopedists also treat congenital defects (such as a misaligned hip) and hereditary diseases (such as muscular dystrophy, which produces muscle weakness and sometimes requires orthopedic procedures for stabilization of the joints).

Although orthopedic surgeons are trained to operate, they do so only on occasion. More common treatments include medication, exercise, or physical therapy.

Orthopedic surgery is a field undergoing changes at a rapid rate. An orthopedist practicing in 1988 pointed out that half the operations he performed were unheard of 18 years earlier when he entered the field. One new development is arthroscopic surgery, usually performed on athletes with torn cartilage in their leg. In arthroscopic surgery, the doctor inserts a tiny instrument into small nicks in the leg and repairs the tears instead of making a large incision. This technique enables the athlete to be treated as an outpatient, free to go home shortly after the operation. Previously—indeed, until the mid-1970s—the patient would have spent a week in the hospital.

Another new development is an allograft, whereby cancerous bone is replaced with bone taken from another human being or from a cadaver and connected to a blood supply. Yet another breakthrough in is the replacement of real joints with artificial ones.

After medical school, orthopedic surgeons must complete a five-year residency. Sixty percent then continue another year of fellowship training in a subspecialty, often dealing with a particular part of the body such as the spine, shoulder, hip, foot, or ankle.

PODIATRY

Podiatrists treat foot diseases and disorders. They are not M.D.s, but most are college graduates who, after four years of podiatric study, are awarded a doctor of podiatric medicine degree. Many superficial foot problems, such as corns and callouses, are handled routinely. However, properly trained and licensed podiatr-

CAREERS IN HEALTH CARE

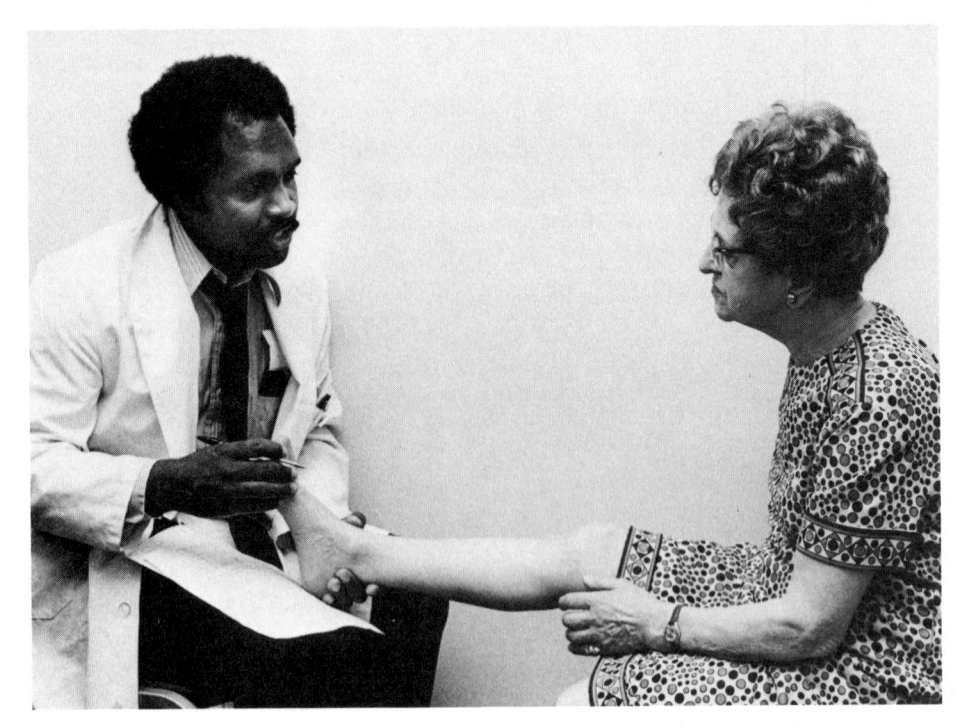

Although they are not M.D.s, podiatrists must complete a four-year medical program. Many go on to perform surgery, often for the removal of bunions (abnormal swellings at the base of the big toe).

ists can also perform surgery. One common type of podiatric surgery is the removal of bunions, abnormal swellings of the joint at the base of the big toe.

DERMATOLOGY

Dermatologists diagnose and treat diseases of the skin, hair, and nails. Because skin covers the entire body, dermatologists must be prepared to work with other specialists. For example, a dermatologist might work with an ophthalmologist concerning eye diseases or a gynecologist in connection with a vaginal irritation. Dermatologists serve a one-year general residency in pediatrics, general medicine, or surgery, followed by a three-year residency in dermatology.

In a recent survey cited in the pamphlet "Your Skin and Your Dermatologist," published in 1987 by the American Academy of

Dermatologists (AAD), acne led the list of the problems they treated most frequently, accounting for nearly 20% of all cases. Next came contact dermatitis, a general term referring to skin diseases resulting from external causes such as poison ivy and industrial and household chemicals. Other common skin problems are cancer, warts, fungal infections, and psoriasis, a skin disorder characterized by red patches with thick, dry, silvery scales.

Dermatologists treat skin problems with lotions, medications, and surgery. In fact, a dermatologist does more minor surgery—usually in the office—than many other surgeons. Surgery is sometimes needed to prevent or provide early control of disease; to improve the skin's appearance by removing growths or discolorations caused by aging, birth, sunlight, or disease; or to establish a definitive diagnosis by removing a part of the skin and analyzing it in the laboratory. Dermatologists provide almost all their treatment during office hours; it is a specialty with few emergencies.

UROLOGY

Urology is an organ-system specialization, treating the urinary system—kidneys, bladder, and external organs—of men and women and the reproductive system in men. Urology is both a medical and surgical specialty.

The most common urological problems involve conditions that hamper the proper drainage of urine. These range from bladder infections to enlargement of the prostate gland (the gland in men that surrounds the neck of the bladder and the urethra), which is treated either by surgical removal or by medication.

Urologists also treat kidney stones, mineral buildups that block the kidney and thus impede urine flow. In this case, urologists combine surgery and medicine; they remove the stone surgically and, when they find what caused the stone, treat the disorder chemically to prevent further stones from forming.

Urologists also help children born with malformations of the genitourinary tract and, of late, have begun teaming up with nephrologists (kidney specialists) to perform kidney transplants.

Because they deal with the male reproductive system, urologists treat—both physically and psychologically—impotence and other sexual problems. They also perform vasectomies, sterilizing operations in which a part of the *vas deferens*, the tube that brings sperm from the testicles to the scrotum, is removed. Vasectomies are usually performed in the doctor's office under local anesthesia. Urologists also perform the delicate microsurgery in which this operation is reversed, although not always successfully.

Urologists complete a total of five years of residency training: three in urology and two in a different field, usually surgery.

• • • •

CHAPTER 5
MAJOR MEDICAL SPECIALTIES

A psychologist (left) meets with a patient.

Physicians with medical specialties diagnose illnesses and treat them with drugs and hormones. They also recommend that patients change their habits by taking more exercise and improving their diet. Medical specialists usually provide more long-term care than surgical specialists provide. At the same time, they recognize their treatments often will not cure a given disease but will only manage it so that the patient can live as normal a life as possible.

PSYCHIATRY AND MENTAL HEALTH

According to the American Psychiatric Association (APA), in any six-month period, one person in five suffers a diagnosable mental disorder. These maladies are treated by professionals who belong to many different categories of mental-health professionals. The physicians who diagnose, treat, and work to prevent mental illness and emotional problems are psychiatrists.

Psychiatrists examine patients to see if there are physical causes for their mental problems. Because they are licensed physicians, psychiatrists are the only mental-health professionals allowed to prescribe drugs.

The two most common mental problems are depression and anxiety. Clinical depression—depression that requires treatment—is characterized by feelings of sadness, helplessness, hopelessness, and irritability that persist for more than two weeks. Depression sometimes leads to anxiety disorders, which often occur on their own. These, according to the APA, are characterized by "an unpleasant and overriding mental tension that has no apparent identifiable cause."

Many teenagers suffer from depression so severe that they become suicidal. Indeed, suicide is the third leading cause of death among teenagers. Psychiatrists are often called upon to help adolescents avoid this tragedy. Treatment can make a huge difference. According to the APA, "With adequate treatment, 80–90% of all depressed people begin to get better within a month."

Other mental illnesses include manic-depressive psychosis, wherein the patient experiences wild mood swings from uncontrollable elation to deep depression; schizophrenia, characterized by delusions, hallucinations, or thought disorders that prevent the patient from coping with normal life; and phobias, a form of anxiety that burdens the patient with irrational and debilitating fears. A common phobia is agoraphobia, the fear of being in open or public places. People who suffer from it find it impossible to leave their homes even for short periods of time. Psychiatrists also treat patients who are dependent on alcohol or drugs or who overeat compulsively.

Psychologists usually have Ph.D. degrees, although people with a master's degree in social work may also practice psychotherapy. There are also art, music, and dance therapists who use nonverbal expression to help patients understand and solve mental and emotional problems. These professions require a master's degree as well.

RADIOLOGY

Radiology is a medical specialty defined by the methods and tools of its practitioners. Radiologists use X rays and other penetrating radiation for one of two purposes. The first is to produce images—often similar to photographic negatives—that enable the radiologist to see inside the body and thus diagnose disease and broken bones. The second is to use strong doses of the penetrating radiation, such as that produced using cobalt, gold, and iodine, to destroy the cells that make up a cancerous tumor. It is possible to do this without killing normal cells because the healthy cells are more resistant to radiation than the tumor cells.

Radiotherapy is limited almost exclusively to treating different types of cancer, where it is used either in addition to or as a substitute for surgery. But radiation diagnosis is useful for many different diseases, including pneumonia, tuberculosis, inflammatory tissue diseases such as arthritis, and broken or sprained bones.

During diagnosis, the radiologist consults with other physicians about the area to be x-rayed. And during radiation treatment, the radiologist needs guidance in determining the size and frequency of cell-destroying dosages.

Recent strides in radiation technology have been enormous. It is now possible for specialists to obtain an image of every part of the body in extremely precise detail. One method, computerized axial tomography (known as CAT scanning), can produce images one centimeter (a third of an inch) wide of any section of the body.

Sonography is another important development, often used to observe the fetus in its early stages of development. Sonography uses ultrasound to penetrate the body of the pregnant woman, specifically the abdominal and pelvic area, and then produce images.

One of the newest developments in radiology is magnetic resonance imaging (MRI), which uses magnetized protons and

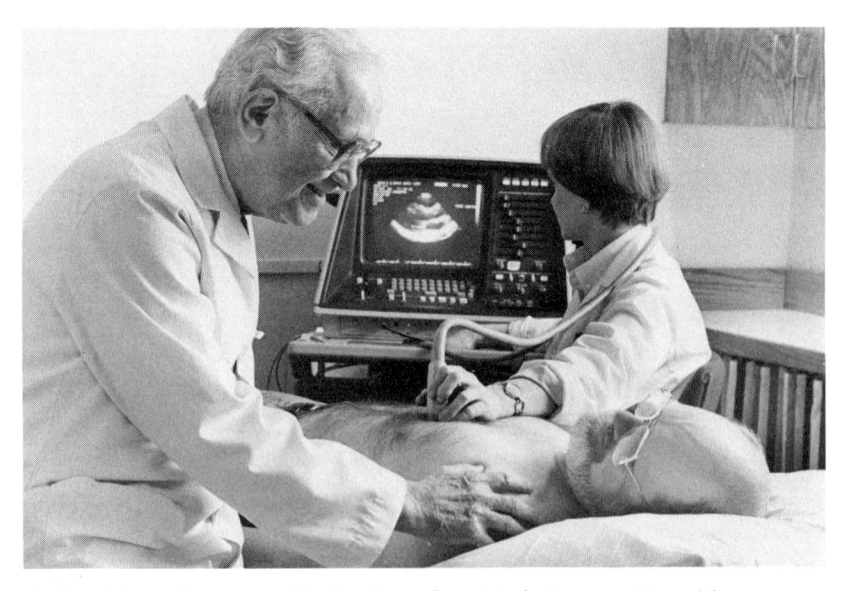

A physician relaxes a patient whose heart is being monitored by a sonogram. Sonarography is especially useful for examining the fetus inside a pregnant woman.

radio-frequency pulses to create images of several levels in the body. These images allow the trained radiologist to discover diseased tissue within the body.

The equipment radiologists use is extremely expensive, ranging from $70,000 for a sonographic unit to $2 million for an MRI unit. Because of this expense, radiologists usually work in hospitals, which can best afford these costly machines.

Radiologists must be familiar with the anatomy and physiology of every organ, as well as with the patterns produced in each by different diseases. They should also be able to correlate this knowledge with what is seen on an X ray or other diagnostic film. Finally, radiologists must master the intricacies of their equipment, understanding not only how it operates but also its shortcomings and possible breakdowns.

A radiologist with a private practice, or one who runs the diagnostic or therapeutic service in a hospital, must supervise a staff composed of other radiologists, radiation-therapy technologists (who hold a two-year degree in the field), diagnostic medical sonographers (who complete a two-year training program plus some college science courses), and receptionists.

Radiologists do not spend a great deal of time with patients.

The technologists usually produce the image; the radiologist's expertise lies in interpreting it.

ANESTHESIOLOGY

Anesthesiologists use a variety of drugs and gases to keep patients comfortable and free from harm during surgery. At the same time, they must make sure the patient's airways remain open so that breathing is possible.

An anesthesiologist typically works on four to five operations a day. Each operation begins with a preoperative examination of the patient and his or her records, followed by a discussion with the patient of the anesthesia that will be used. The anesthesiologist also tells the nurses on the floor how to medicate the patient so he or she is somewhat sedated before reaching the operating room.

In the operating room and before the surgeon arrives, the anesthesiologist sets up the gas-administering machinery—if gas will be used—and also the monitoring equipment that will indicate the patient's heartbeat, pulse rate, and blood oxygen level. These machines sound an alarm if any of these vital signs falls to a dangerously low level. At the appropriate time, the anesthesiologist administers the anesthesia. Once the operation ends, the specialist monitors the patient on his or her way to the recovery room or the intensive care unit and remains there until the anesthesia appears to be wearing off and care can be turned over to the nurses.

The type of anesthesia given during the operation depends mainly on the type of surgery to be performed, though it also varies according to the allergies and general condition of the patient. Common forms of anesthesia are intravenous injection of barbiturates, used for superficial procedures such as biopsies of breast tissue or the removal of growths from the feet; inhalation agents, administered continuously through a hollow tube in the tracheal airway—the nose or mouth—and continually controlled by the anesthesiologist, used most often for chest and abdominal surgery; and regional anesthetics, injections that block off a specific area, such as the pelvis and lower back during delivery of a baby.

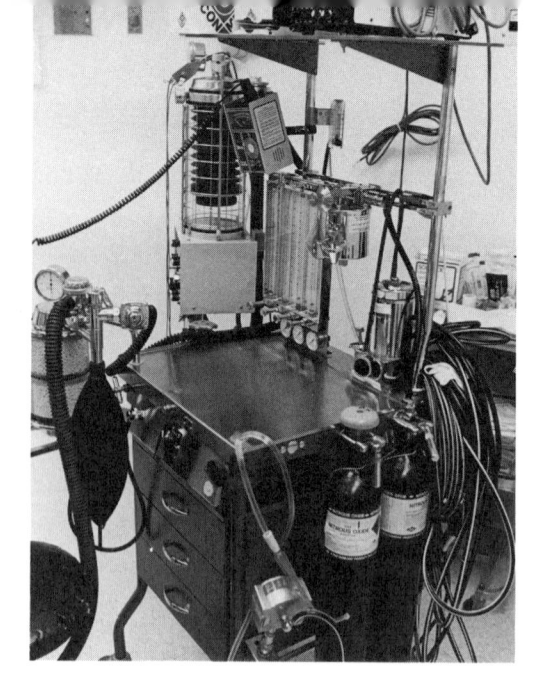

This anesthesiology cart, designed for use during surgery, includes equipment that monitors the patient's heartbeat, pulse rate, and blood oxygen level and machinery that dispenses nitrous oxide.

SPORTS MEDICINE

The category of sports medicine includes a group of careers, each concerned with a different aspect of the health and well-being of athletes, from amateur joggers to professional football players.

The physicians who handle a sports team's illnesses and injuries are most often a family practitioner or internist, and a consulting orthopedic surgeon. The practitioner or internist performs the physical exams and treats less serious injuries. The orthopedist treats the major injuries of the musculoskeletal system, performs surgery if necessary, and supervises the patient's rehabilitation and return to play. Both physicians cooperate to devise methods of team practice, play, and conditioning that can reduce the number of injuries suffered by athletes.

These physicians supervise physiotherapists, whose task is to effect the physical rehabilitation of athletes recovering from injuries or illnesses affecting the nerves, muscles, or bones. They must complete a four-year course leading to a bachelor's degree in physical therapy.

NEUROLOGY

Neurology is the medical specialty that deals with disorders of the nervous system, which includes the brain, spinal cord, and peripheral nerves (the motor and sensory nerves apart from the brain and spinal cord). Neurology also deals with muscular disorders that can stem from defects in the nervous system. This is the most complex organ system in the body, with millions of synapses (places where a nerve signal jumps from one cell to another). The challenge of understanding this system is what draws most neurologists to the specialty.

An array of illnesses causes patients to visit neurologists. The most common symptom is the headache, particularly migraine headaches, which are extremely severe ailments often attended by visual problems, nausea, and vomiting. A major disease treated by neurologists is multiple sclerosis, which strikes young adults. It is caused by abnormal destruction of the sheaths surrounding nerves in the brain and spinal cord. Another fairly common neurological disease is epilepsy, which is marked by abnormal electrical activity in brain tissue. Its sufferers are afflicted with an uncontrollable shaking in the arms and legs or, during a seizure, loss of consciousness.

Neurologists often treat older patients, many of whom have suffered a stroke, a blockage of one of the major arteries leading to the brain that can cause impairment of brain function. Neurologists also treat Alzheimer's disease, a complicated, not yet fully understood breakdown in mental functions eventually resulting in death.

A large and complex part of a neurologist's work is making accurate diagnoses. In fact, before dramatic breakthroughs occurred in pharmacology (the science of drugs), making a correct diagnosis was almost all neurologists could do to help patients. Although diagnosis remains a critical function, there is now the possibility of effective treatment for some diseases.

The newest advances in neurology involve research into the genetics of such diseases as Alzheimer's and muscular dystrophy, a wasting of muscle tissue that leaves the accompanying nerve tissue intact. As research progresses, neurologists hope eventually to be able to intervene and supply the genetic material whose absence is causing the disease.

CARDIOLOGY

Cardiologists treat two types of diseases and malfunctions: those of the heart and those of the vessels that carry blood to and from the heart.

A condition commonly treated by cardiologists is a myocardial infarction, known as a heart attack. This is the death of a segment of heart tissue following interruption of its blood supply. A heart attack may occur when one of the blood vessels supplying the heart is blocked, often by a part of the blood-vessel wall that has degenerated and impedes the flow of blood.

Cardiologists also treat heart failure, which happens when the heart's pumping mechanism fails to pump fluid out of the lungs adequately. Congestion results, and the patient cannot breathe. Another common ailment is high blood pressure, which occurs when the flow of blood places too much stress on the vessels or the heart. A prime cause of this condition is arteriosclerosis (hardening of the arteries). Cardiologists also deal with problems of irregular heart rhythm, called arrhythmia.

Cardiologists treat many of these problems with sophisticated new drugs. These include calcium channel blockers (which relieve spasms of the coronary arteries) and diuretics (which relieve the load on the heart by reducing congestion in the lungs and promote the formation and release of urine). Another drug, digitalis, is a derivative of the foxglove plant that has been used for centuries to strengthen the heartbeat. New diagnostic techniques have also aided cardiologists who work in hospitals. One such technique is the angiogram. During this procedure, dye is injected into the blood vessels, and by examining the progress of the dye by taking films doctors can see how the vessels work. These films indicate whether there are arterial spasms and if the vessels are narrowed or blocked, which may eventually lead to a heart attack.

Cardiologists cooperate closely with heart surgeons. The surgeon actually operates to correct a malfunction, but only after the cardiologist has made the diagnosis and helped decide on the degree and location of the problem. After the operation is completed, both physicians continue to care for the patient. The surgeon checks the progress of the wound—is it healing? are liquids draining properly?—whereas the cardiologist prescribes any medication that might be needed to stabilize the heartbeat or thin the blood.

Major Medical Specialties

PHARMACOLOGY

Pharmacology, the study of drugs, is a branch of medicine. Most pharmacologists are not M.D.s, however, but Ph.D.s. Pharmacologists do not treat patients. Instead they develop new drugs, try to discover more about the properties of known drugs, and study the effects on the body of chemical substances in the environment.

Three-quarters of America's pharmacologists are employed in nonprofit institutions such as universities and the government. As they develop or investigate drugs, these specialists try to discover the relationship between dose and effect, the ways in which the drug is absorbed, transformed, and eliminated, and the adverse as well as the beneficial effects of the medication. Some pharmacologists test the safety of food and other products, including pesticides and detergents, which may be eaten accidentally, often by children.

PUBLIC HEALTH

Public-health-care workers try to improve the well-being of entire communities. Their varied activities include mounting cam-

A teacher helps two students in a pharmacy lab. Pharmacologists are not doctors but researchers who develop new drugs, explore the properties of known drugs, and study the effects of chemical substances.

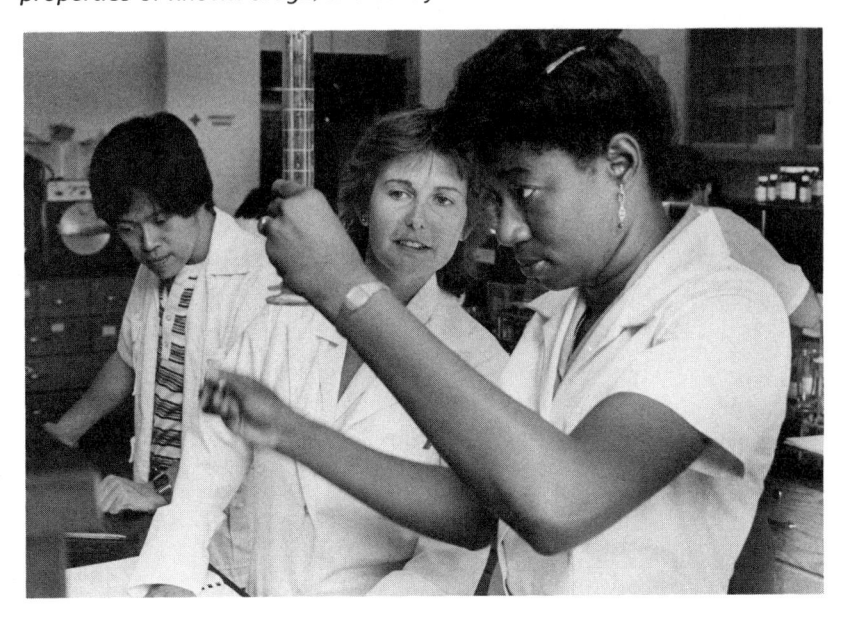

paigns to stop smoking, devising ads urging the use of condoms as a way to prevent the spread of AIDS, sponsoring artists who design posters encouraging pregnant women to see a doctor, and acting in other ways to educate the public.

People who work in public health are not necessarily M.D.s. Often they have completed special graduate programs in public health and have a Ph.D., master of science, or master or doctor of public health degree.

Public-health officials often work for government agencies. The largest of these is the Public Health Service, which is part of the U.S. Department of Health and Human Services. The Public Health Service's many subsidiary organizations include the following:

1. National Institutes of Health (NIH). The NIH's mission is to help scientists learn more about the life processes that underlie health and to improve methods of preventing, diagnosing, and treating disease. It sponsors research conducted in its own laboratories just outside Washington, D.C., and funds researchers working in other laboratories.

2. Centers for Disease Control (CDC). The CDC, located in Atlanta, Georgia, works to prevent and control infectious and chronic diseases, to reduce health hazards in the environment and the workplace, and to educate the public about health risks and the means of avoiding them.

3. Alcohol, Drug Abuse, and Mental Health Administration (ADAMHA). The ADAMHA conducts research in its own laboratories and funds research in other laboratories. Its agenda includes rooting out the causes of substance abuse and finding ways to reduce it along with its allied health problems.

4. Food and Drug Administration (FDA). The FDA conducts laboratory research and makes about 50,000 inspections a year to make sure that foods are both safe and nourishing, that drugs and medical devices are safe and effective, that cosmetics do not harm the user, that radiation-emitting products are not dangerous to those who use them, and that all these products are fully and accurately labeled.

OCCUPATIONAL MEDICINE

Specialists in occupational medicine focus on the health of workers, usually by caring for employees at particular companies. Some specialists also teach and carry out research.

Like people who work in public health, occupational physicians generate large-scale health-promotion activities, such as antismoking campaigns or—by supervising cafeteria services—improving diets in the workplace. The physician whose office is located at a factory or office building can monitor health problems such as high blood pressure through regular follow-up examinations.

Other ways in which occupational medicine specialists may promote health care include the following:

1. Ensuring that new employees are physically and emotionally suited to handle their work.

2. Helping to provide a safe work environment as established by the guidelines created by the 1970 federal Occupational Safety and Health Act.

3. Helping workers injured on the job to get prompt and appropriate medical attention—guaranteed through state workers compensation laws.

4. Mobilizing a speedy response to emergency medical situations that occur at the workplace.

5. Consulting with workers at the early stage of illness, when it is most treatable. Many employees will consult the company doctor rather than a private practitioner because they are reluctant to lose time on the job. Also, the company doctor can make a diagnosis that takes into account the potential health hazards of the patient's work environment.

Occupational physicians often run an employee-assistance program through which counselors and social workers advise employees about sources for assistance in dealing with psychological, marital, family, financial, alcohol, and drug abuse problems.

CAREERS IN HEALTH CARE

Most practitioners of occupational medicine have specialized in internal or family medicine, psychiatry, or general surgery. Because there are few formal residencies in the field, their extra training comes in special courses and through firsthand experience.

ALTERNATIVE SPECIALTIES: CHIROPRACTIC MEDICINE AND HOLISTIC MEDICINE

Chiropractic Medicine

A doctor of chiropractic medicine is a health-care professional who believes that human well-being depends on the relationship between structure and function in the human body. Chiropractors pay special attention to spinal mechanics (the science of movement) and musculoskeletal, neurological, vascular (blood vessel), and nutritional relationships. Chiropractors are licensed in all 50 states and in Puerto Rico and must complete 2 years of

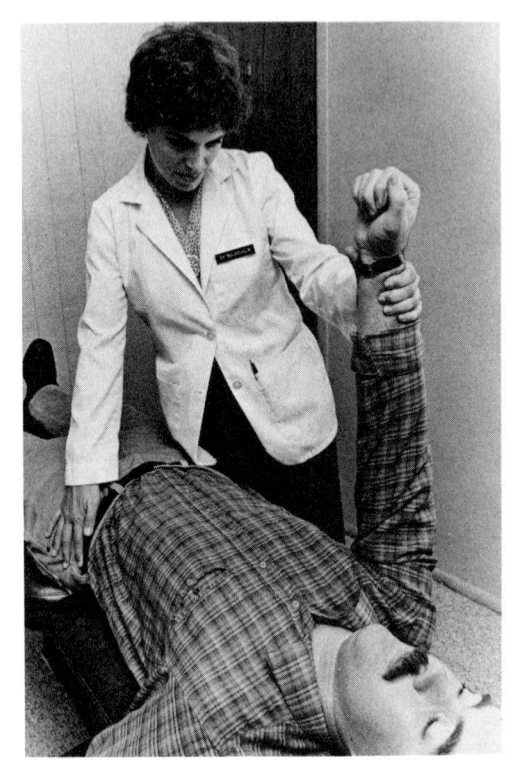

A chiropractor tests a patient's arm movement. Chiropractic holds that many ailments stem from the faulty alignment of a person's musculoskeletal system.

A holistic doctor tests a patient. Holistic medicine, which has gained influence in recent years, deals with the whole person, weighing physical, mental, emotional, spiritual, and environmental factors.

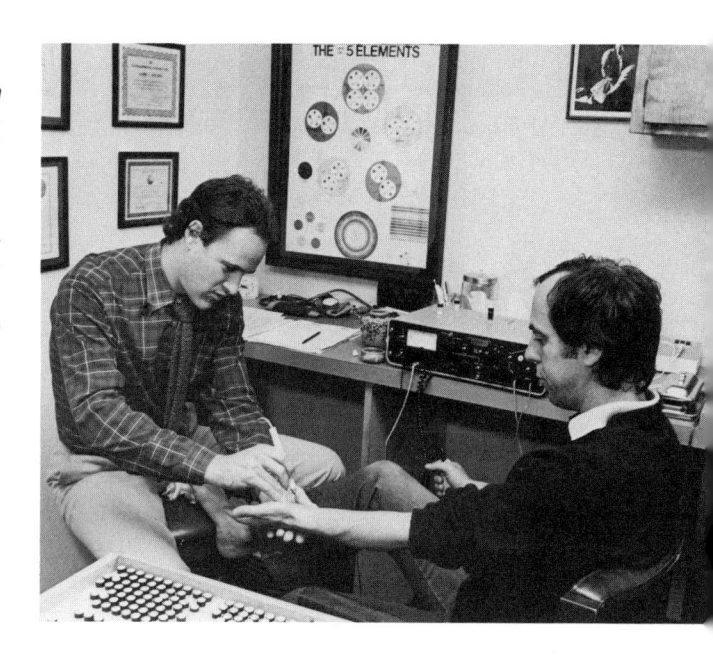

prechiropractic college work after high school in addition to a 4-year course in an accredited chiropractic college. This course concentrates on basic science for the first two years and practical treatment and diagnosis (half of it done in clinics) for the final two years.

Chiropractic medicine is built upon the theory that disease may be caused by disturbances of the nervous system, disturbances which in turn may be caused by subluxation (misalignment) of the musculoskeletal structure.

Chiropractic doctors do not prescribe drugs or perform surgery. Their methods of treatment include recommending vitamin and mineral supplements, offering advice on how to form healthier habits and develop better posture, and—most important—performing structural adjustment, a precise, delicate maneuvering that requires bioengineering skills. This adjustment is often followed by physical therapy.

Holistic Medicine

Holistic medicine deals with the whole person, taking into account the physical, mental, emotional, spiritual, and environmental aspects of the person's life. This form of medicine places as much emphasis on education for wellness as on treatment for illness.

Practitioners of holistic medicine must be licensed by the states in which they work. Traditionally, they have been trained in one of the alternative primary-care specialties, such as chiropractic medicine, but they have developed ideas that differ from those of conventional medical practice. Holistic doctors usually practice as part of a group that may include an acupuncturist (a person trained in therapy for relieving pain or changing a function of the body based on inserting needles in precise places in the body); a nutritionist; an exercise physiologist; a psychological counselor; a naturopath (naturopathy is a system of treating disease using natural foods, light, warmth, massage, regular exercise, and the avoidance of drugs); and a massage therapist.

The two basic ideas underlying holistic theory are that the mind exerts great control over the health of the body and that interaction between doctor and patient should be based on their cooperation as equals. This differs from the traditional model in which the doctor is the authority and decides what treatment the patient will undergo without the patient's participation in the decision. In order to emphasize the concept of patient responsibility, holistic medicine refers to "consumers" instead of "patients."

For example, a holistic doctor ascertains by examination that the consumer's throat is sore but then, considering the mind-body connection, goes on to ask, "Why are you getting sore throats?" The doctor then explores the patient's nutrition, habits, and psychological attitudes.

Before treating high blood pressure with drugs, as many cardiologists would, a holistic doctor might ask a consumer to practice biofeedback (a method used in learning to alter certain functions of the body through relaxation), exercise, and meditation to reduce the tension that could be causing blood vessels to constrict and thus raise pressure.

• • • •

CHAPTER 6

CAREERS IN NURSING

Nursing is so varied that it is difficult to define. According to one registered nurse, "Nursing is the art and science dedicated to compassionate concern for maintaining and promoting health, preventing illness, and caring for and rehabilitating the members of our society."

REGISTERED NURSING

Registered nursing requires perhaps the most education of any area of nursing, offers the highest salary, and encompasses many different careers. It can include the flight nurse who flies by helicopter to pick up a heart attack victim from a remote area or the psychiatric nurse practitioner who runs his or her own private practice. Despite this variety, however, there is a common educational standard met by most nurses, which can be built upon or drawn from when moving from one area of the field to another.

Karen Ballard's nursing career offers a good example. Karen received a master's degree in child psychiatric nursing. As a child psychiatric nurse, she worked first with schizophrenic children, then with young leukemia patients, helping them adjust to their illness and the consequences of treatment, such as loss of hair. At the same time she was responsible for explaining the illness, along with its treatment and side effects, to teachers and students, so that children well enough to reenter school could do so smoothly.

After leaving that job, Karen then became a critical-care nurse. She worked with surgical patients in a hospital setting and then became a family nurse, helping people adjust to the illness that gripped their loved ones. Later, she moved into community health and education as a public-health nurse, at the same time teaching courses in psychiatric nursing. Karen is now the director of the Nursing Practice and Services Program of the New York State Nurses Association.

Successful nurses, according to Karen Ballard, must be well organized and able to stay calm and confident even in the midst of a crisis. They must keep abreast of new developments in the rapidly changing health field. But they must also be gentle and caring. Nurses must be willing to receive scant thanks for their labors, content in the knowledge that they have helped someone who needed them.

Education for Registered Nursing

There are currently three ways to become a registered nurse (RN): through completion of a four-year bachelor of science program at a college or university; through a two-year associate degree program at a community or junior college, technical institute or university; or through a diploma program, two to three years long, given by hospitals and independent schools of nursing.

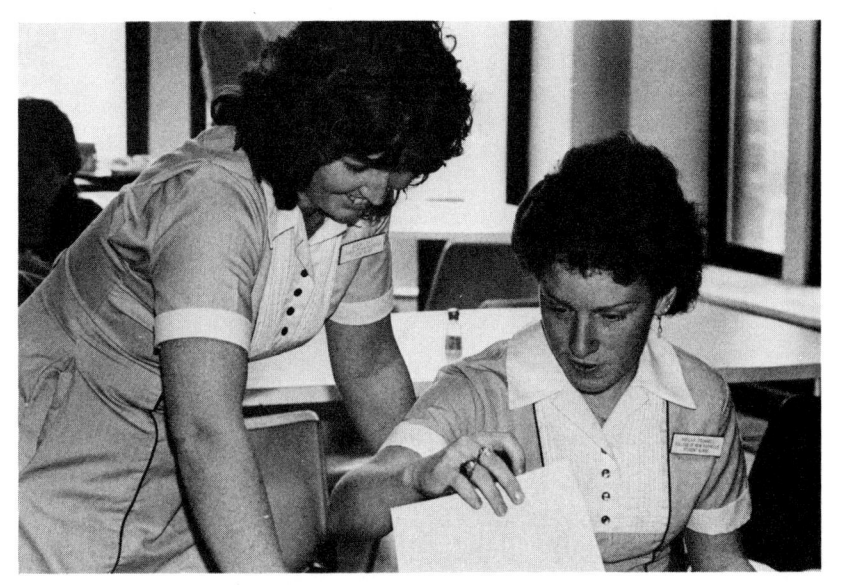

Nursing students confer before a class. A wide array of careers is open to nurses, who now play a larger role than ever before in the human side of health care.

The American Nurses' Association, most individual state organizations, and independent leaders in the field are lobbying for all 50 states to pass legislation requiring all registered nurses entering the field to have a bachelor's degree. They want to eliminate nonacademic diploma programs and to use associate degree programs for training licensed practical or vocational nurses. Such legislation may become a reality in most states by 1995.

Advocates of this requirement argue that registered nursing is an enormously complicated field, defined by rapidly changing technological advances and demanding proficiency in such areas as cross-cultural communication and management and budgeting skills. They think the full development of these skills requires a four-year college degree program. Advocates also see the bachelor's degree—already a requirement for advancement to specialized, managerial, and teaching positions—as a means to attract and retain more nurses. The degree might also help address the main reasons for the nursing shortage: dissatisfaction with working conditions, the lack of attention given to nurses in health-care decision making, the lack of respect nurses receive from other health-care professionals, and comparatively low salaries.

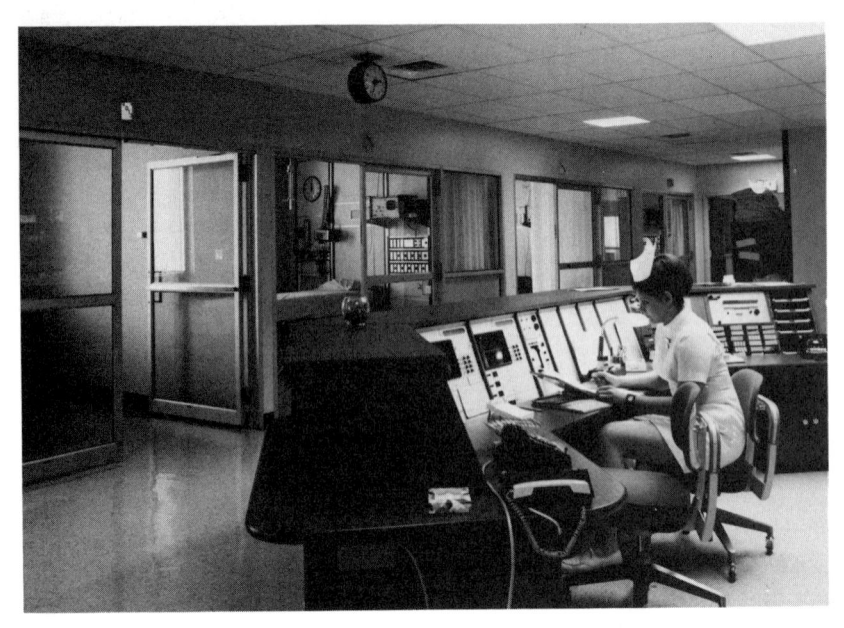

A nurse on duty at an intensive care unit (ICU), a setting in which a crisis can occur at any hour of the day. Nurses must remain calm and confident and be prepared to work long past their designated shifts.

The average nurse's salary is expected to rise from $25,000 in the mid-1980s to $50,000 in the year 2000. Unfortunately, the shortage will also increase the burden that already weighs down overworked nurses.

People commonly train to become RNs in the following ways: **Bachelor's Degree Program:** The four-year program includes extensive course work in the natural sciences, such as chemistry and biology, and the social sciences, such as sociology and psychology. Professional nursing courses feature nursing theory, which is then applied through clinical laboratory experience in hospitals, community-health agencies, and other health-care institutions.

Like medical students, nursing students follow grueling schedules and must master a great deal of difficult material. In addition, they often complete long clinical sessions. For this reason, many students seek out nursing programs and universities affiliated with a particular hospital that offers clinical experience.

Their choice of programs often depends on tuition costs, which vary from school to school and from state to state. State universities, as a rule, costs less than private institutions, especially if the student is an official resident of that state.

Associate Degree Programs: Associate degree programs last two years and include course work in basic science, in communication skills, and in the theory and practice of technical nursing. Students also receive supervised experience with patients, which prepares them to assume staff nurse positions in acute and chronic health-care facilities. These programs are often offered at community and junior colleges and can be quite inexpensive for local residents.

Diploma Programs: Diploma programs are given by hospitals and independent nursing schools. They include the study of nursing theory and offer students the opportunity to gain practical experience through supervised work with patients. The diploma curriculum also features courses in the biological, social, and physical sciences, available at colleges for academic credit.

Registration and Certification: Each state has a board that governs the licensing and registration of nurses. Applicants must complete an approved two- or four-year program and pass an examination. In addition, the American Nurses' Association recognizes 19 specialties for which it awards an additional professional credential of certification. Certification requires additional education, training, or experience beyond that required for an RN and is granted after passage of an examination made up by nurses in the specialty area.

Registered Nursing Careers

Nurse Midwives As independent practitioners, nurse midwives do not necessarily work under the supervision of a physician. They care for essentially healthy women and newborns before, during, and after delivery, often working in freestanding birthing centers. Nurse midwives are RNs, usually after completing a four-year college program, and also hold an advanced degree.

Neonatal Nursing One of the most dramatic kinds of nursing is provided by the neonatal nurse, who cares for newborn infants. Modern technology can now save 80% of all infants born up to two months premature. It is the neonatal nurses who apply

A Day in the Life of a Neonatal Nurse

At 7:00 P.M., Stephanie Arrow arrives at the large New Jersey hospital where she works in the neonatal intensive care unit (NICU). Before entering the NICU, she changes into her uniform and then "scrubs up"—washes thoroughly: Any germ or infection picked up by the infants she works with can tip the scales against them in their struggle to survive.

Stephanie enters the NICU and consults with the nurse whose shift has now ended. This nurse gives a report on the infants Stephanie will be responsible for tonight. Stephanie learns if the babies are to be fed and how often, how much oxygen they should receive, and how the IVs are running and when they must be changed. (IVs are intravenous injections, usually of glucose, that nourish the body when it is not able to take in solid food; the apparatus is used to administer medication continuously and in controlled amounts.)

Once the nurse concludes her report, Stephanie double-checks it against the orders written by a doctor on the babies' charts. "It's always necessary to check the doctor's orders," Stephanie explains. "Not that you don't trust your fellow nurses—it's just that things can get confusing when you're handling more than one baby."

For the next 12 hours, Stephanie will care for 2 infants. One, hooked up to an IV, needs to be checked only every 2 hours and to have its IV changed as needed. The second baby—in semistable condition on a respirator (a machine that "breathes" for the baby)—requires more care. Every two hours it must be suctioned, that is, have the mucus removed from its airways. Stephanie must also check the setting on the respirator, register the blood-gas level, and change the baby's two IVs. Babies on respirators often have one IV placed in either an arm or a leg and another in the umbilical artery. Two IVs give the physician access, if necessary, to arteries as well as veins.

In addition to handling these tasks, Stephanie must call each baby's doctor with a report on the respective infant's vital signs. She communicates this information every four hours, unless the baby's condition suddenly changes, in

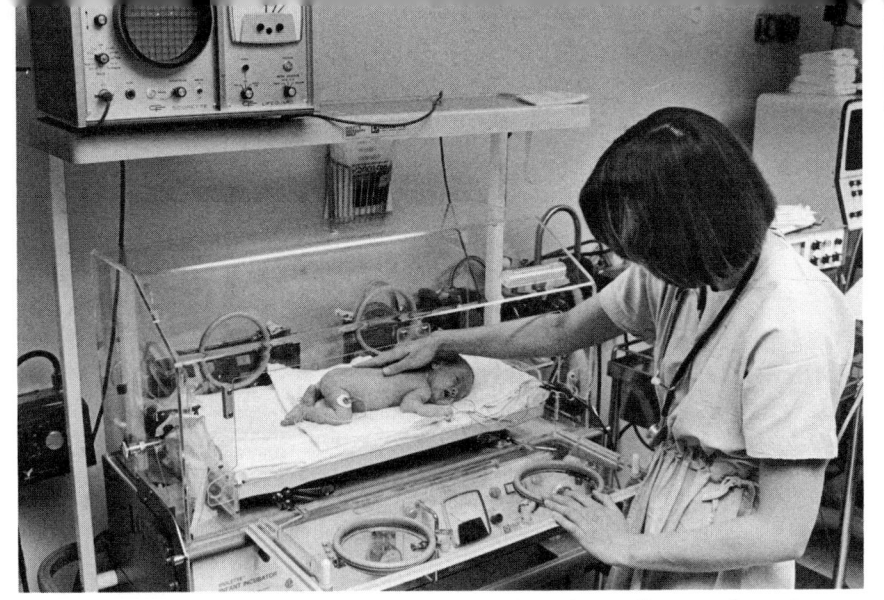

A neonatal nurse cares for a premature newborn kept alive inside an incubator. Modern technology has enabled health-care workers to save 80% of all infants born up to 2 months before they are due.

which case Stephanie will immediately alert the physician. "There are times when one of your babies will 'crash' and you have to perform life-saving measures right away and turn the care of your other infants over to another nurse. Even then, the emergency situation might last for hours—well past the duration of your shift. You have no choice but to see the emergency through. This is not a job where you can say good night and go home just because your time is up. If one of the infants you're caring for is struggling for his life, you're right there with him. In NICU there is no difference between day and night. The babies don't recognize any difference and, consequently, neither do the nurses working with them."

At the end of her 12-hour shift, Stephanie reports on the babies' condition to the nurse who replaces her and prepares to go home. It has been a long shift. There have been no miraculous recoveries, but the babies have remained stable.

"I guess a lot of people think of doctors and nurses as performing 'miracles'—making split-second decisions that save lives. And, in fact, that does happen a lot. When it does, it's a great feeling for all of us. But there are other times when even the most heroic efforts are not enough. For example, you may revive and stabilize a baby, only to find out he's sustained severe brain damage. For that reason, my greatest concern is improving the quality of life of some infants. If I can believe I've helped just one infant, then my job is a little less frustrating, a little less heart-breaking, and a lot more rewarding."

that technology around-the-clock—often working in a ratio of one nurse to one infant.

Neonatal nurses must be familiar with various types of technology, including heart/lung and kidney dialysis machines. Unfortunately, although these machines can keep the baby alive, they may also produce tragic side effects, such as blindness or mental retardation.

The neonatal nurse is not only responsible for the infants in his or her care but, to some extent, for their parents as well. He or she must explain to the parents exactly what type of care their infant is receiving and what the possible consequences are. In the event that the infant's life is in danger or that he or she has been declared either brain dead or beyond the help of physicians, the neonatal nurse must clarify for the parents the options permitted by state law. Often, this means giving them all the information they need to decide whether to continue the baby's life-support systems.

Neonatal nurses also try to educate future mothers on the dangers of cigarette smoking and alcohol and drug abuse, which often cause babies to be born prematurely or with problems such as fetal alcohol syndrome or drug withdrawal. Extensive abuse of many drugs can cause severe birth defects as well.

Emergency Nursing Emergency nurses diagnose and begin treatment of urgent and acute physical or psychological problems. This care may range from taping up a sprained ankle to hooking up life-support machines that support a patient's life when his or her heart has stopped pumping. Emergency nurses also respond to victims of physical and psychological violence, such as rape and child abuse.

Emergency nurses work in hospital emergency departments, freestanding emergency-care facilities, and prehospital-care units such as helicopters and ambulances. They must be flexible, able to cope with an uneventful shift followed by a stressful one filled with emergencies. An emergency nurse sees sudden and often senseless death and must be mature enough to deal sensitively with the patient's family during crises.

Operating Room Nursing Operating room nurses—or OR nurses, as they are commonly called—work with doctors and

Careers in Nursing

Emergency nurses working at a busy hospital station. These health-care professionals diagnose and initiate treatment of urgent physiological and psychological problems.

patients before, during, and immediately after surgery. They must achieve a professional rapport with surgeons, anesthesiologists, and other nurses. OR nurses must also deal with patients' families. This can be trying, particularly when the surgery is to take place as a result of an unexpected emergency and the doctor is too busy to soothe family members.

Operating rooms have both scrub and circulating nurses. The circulating nurse is a nonsterile member of the surgical team who connects the operating room to the rest of the hospital, brings tissue to the pathology lab, and relays the lab diagnosis to the surgeon.

The scrub nurse, who remains within the sterile boundaries of the operation, is usually responsible for handing instruments to the surgeon and the surgeon's assistant. In most hospitals, this means the nurse must be familiar with many different operations, must know the instruments, and must know the order in which they are needed.

Nurse Anesthetist According to the American Association of Nurse Anesthetists, some 20 million anesthetics are administered each year in the United States. Nurse anesthetists, under

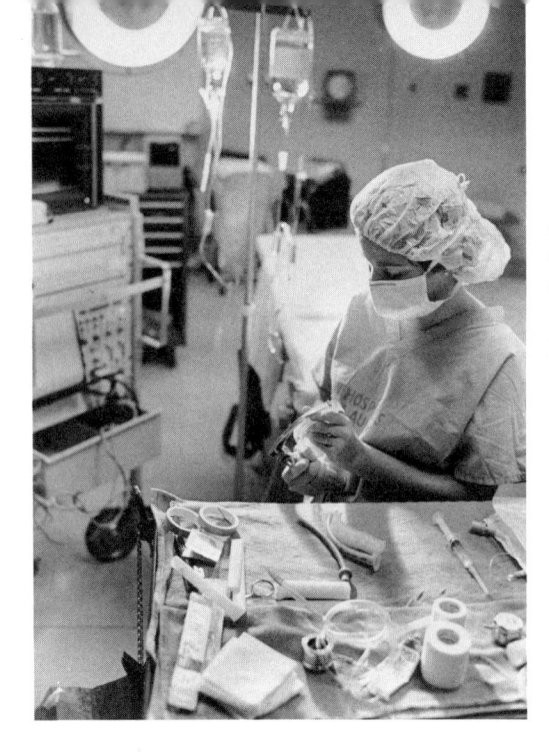

Operating-room staffs include scrub nurses, such as this woman, who lay out instruments before surgery and then hand them to the surgeon during the operation.

the direction of an anesthesiologist, administer half of them. Nurse anesthetists are among the highest-paid nurses in the country, with an average income—in 1984—of $41,093.

Approximately half of all nurse anesthetists work for hospitals. Another 30% are employed by physicians and the remainder are self-employed as free-lance nurse anesthetists.

In addition to or as part of their nursing education, CRNAs (certified registered nurse anesthetists) take 2 years of course work in anesthesia and receive practical experience with 450 different anesthetics over the course of 800 hours. Before they are allowed to practice, nurse anesthetists must pass a national certification examination and complete a continuing education and recertification program every two years.

Pediatric Nursing Pediatric nurses provide health services to children in doctor's offices, hospitals, clinics, and community-health agencies. They may be either associates or nurse practitioners. Nurse practitioners are RNs with special training—often a master's degree. Depending on laws, which vary slightly from one state to another, they may perform and prescribe care independently of a physician. Associates sometimes do the same work under the supervision of a doctor. The work of a pediatric nurse often includes several tasks. They perform physical examinations on healthy children, administer immunizations, and advise families about normal and abnormal child development. They may also manage maladies such as upper respiratory tract infections, rashes, and contagious diseases, as well as chronic illnesses such as diabetes and asthma.

School Nursing School nurses test children for sight, hearing, and growth problems and inform parents of the results, often suggesting clinics and hospitals for follow-up care. In areas of the country with many poor children and uneducated parents, school nurses may provide the services that in more affluent areas are provided by pediatricians during regular office visits. School nurses may tell teachers if health problems are interfering with learning, give classes in health education, and field health questions from students, parents, and school personnel. Another important role of school nurses is responding to student illnesses and making the school system more sensitive to issues of health and wellness.

Military Nursing Military nurses usually work in small, isolated base hospitals, often with no more than 50 beds. These professionals supply a full range of services, including pediatric, medical, and obstetric. Some highly educated and experienced nurses outrank doctors, and because rank matters greatly in the military, nurses and doctors work together as equals more frequently than in civilian life.

Another difference between army and civilian nursing is the ratio of men to women: in civilian life 3% of the nurses are male; in the army 30% of the nurses are male. Moreover, because some specialist physicians, pediatricians for example, are not on duty 24 hours a day, a military nurse may have more responsibility and independence than nurses at larger hospitals.

A nurse in the military has two careers, one as a military officer and the other as a health-care professional. As a military officer, a nurse must take courses in military education and participate in various base activities.

A military nurse must serve at least one three-year term. During a 20-year career, a nurse can expect 2 tours of duty overseas that will last from 15 months to 3 or 4 years. Large military hospitals may have special use for nurses in burn and orthopedic units, plastic surgery, and flight nursing—all part of their ongoing preparation for combat conditions. Army nurses also participate in humanitarian efforts during crises such as earthquakes, plane crashes, and nuclear disasters.

Community Nursing Community nursing is a broad field unified by its emphasis on the health of people outside of institutions such as hospitals and nursing homes. The approach of community nursing is holistic; that is, it looks at the whole person and at the dynamics of the patient's interaction with his family and community. As such, community nursing often deals with social and psychosocial problems.

Community nurses work in a variety of settings. They are often part of a government or private—profit or nonprofit—visiting nurse agency that sends professionals into the homes of people who do not need, or cannot afford, continual nursing. In this setting, the physician sets forth a medical-care plan to be followed by the patient. In order to evaluate how successful the plan will be, the nurse assesses the patient's knowledge and understanding.

Other community nursing sites include storefront clinics in poor neighborhoods and walk-in centers for alcoholics. Community nurses, who are closely related to public-health nurses, may also run health education programs or do tuberculosis screening.

OTHER CAREERS IN NURSING

Licensed Practical Nursing

Licensed practical nurses (LPNs), or licensed vocational nurses, as they are officially known in Texas and California, provide 88% of the country's direct patient care, the other 12% being provided by registered nurses.

LPNs work under the supervision of a physician, registered nurse, or dentist and handle as many aspects of patient care as state law allows. They often record a patient's condition by observation and by taking temperature, blood pressure, and pulse and respiration rates; administer medications and apply com-

A nurse's aide (right) observes as her supervising nurse changes a patient's intravenous apparatus. Nurse's aides bathe and feed patients, change linens, and make beds.

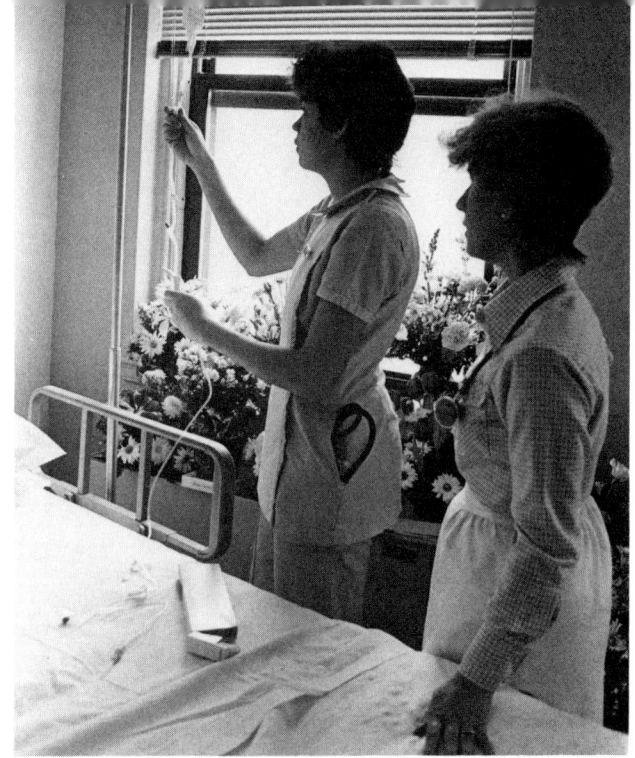

presses, ice bags, and hot water bottles; and bathe, dress, and assist patients who need help walking.

Some LPNs collect routine laboratory specimens, sterilize equipment and supplies, and record their patients' food and fluid intake and output. LPNs may also work with oxygen supplies, catheters (hollow, flexible tubes inserted into a vessel or space in the body to extract or add fluids), and tracheotomy tubes (tubes patients breathe through when a surgical cut has been made in their windpipe to allow air to enter the lungs).

Two-thirds of LPNs work in hospitals, but others work in patients' homes, not only caring for the ill but also cooking and cleaning for them, and instructing other family members on how to perform simple nursing tasks. LPNs also work with elderly residents in nursing homes, where LPNs are the largest group of health workers.

Most LPNs have a high school diploma or equivalent (helpful high school courses include biology, chemistry, psychology, and human relations) and complete a 12-month, full-time course given by many hospitals, technical or vocational schools, 2-year colleges, and a few high schools and 4-year colleges. The program includes course work in anatomy, physiology, pharmacology, nutrition, sociology, and pediatrics. Practical experience includes working with medical and surgical patients and often with patients at psychiatric hospitals and nursing homes. Students often spend five 6:00 A.M. to 8:00 P.M. days in school each week, either in the classroom or doing clinical work.

Costs and arrangements for a licensed practical nurse course vary. Some are free. Others require tuition of more than $1,000. Some programs provide room and board. Others offer no living quarters. There are also correspondence courses in practical nursing, but their graduates do not qualify to take the state licensing examination.

Nursing-related Careers

Home Health Aides: Under the supervision of home-care or social-service agencies, home health aides provide services to homebound or disabled individuals and their families. They perform personal-care nursing tasks, such as bathing the patient, caring for children, or performing household jobs that help create a healthier environment for the person and family. Home health aides usually work for agencies, which prefer mature persons with home- or family-care backgrounds. Once hired, aides receive a brief training program.

Nurse's Aides and Orderlies: The duties of providing basic patient care under direct nursing supervision fall to nurse's aides and orderlies. They may bathe and feed patients, change linens, and make beds. They receive no formal training. However, they may receive six to eight weeks of on-the-job training once they are hired. Most hospitals prefer to hire nurse's aides and orderlies who have a high school diploma.

• • • •

CHAPTER 7

DENTISTRY

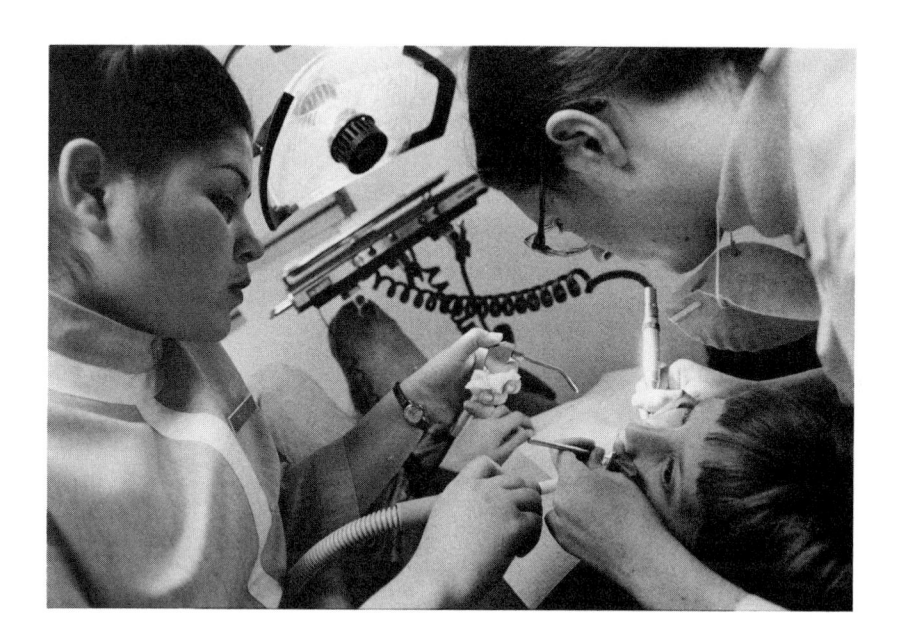

PRIMARY-CARE DENTISTRY

Dentist The main work of dentists used to be "drilling and filling." However, in recent years the use of fluoride and overall improvement in daily care have greatly reduced the incidence of tooth decay. This does not mean that repairing cavities is no longer part of the dentist's job but that other services have come to assume more importance. These include educating the public and individual patients on the nutritional aspects of good oral health and improving a patient's appearance through the use of newly developed techniques. Moreover, as primary-care physicians, dentists often detect the first signs of diseases such as hypertension and cancer.

Dental surgeons perform surgery (actually, filling a cavity is a form of dental surgery), which includes correcting facial and dental deformities caused by accidents or birth defects, and they direct the creation of substitutes, such as dentures (false teeth); bridges, which connect two teeth; and crowns, which rebuild teeth fully or partially lost because of injury or decay.

A typical dentist spends 40% of his day on operative dentistry (fillings and special decay-preventing sealants for children's permanent teeth), 30% on prosthetics (making crowns and bridges to substitute for lost teeth), 20% on root canal work (the removal of diseased nerves and the surrounding tissue), and 10% on periodontal or gum work (trimming and cleaning the gums to improve their condition). When teeth are lost, a dentist must not only decide exactly what type of restoration is needed but must

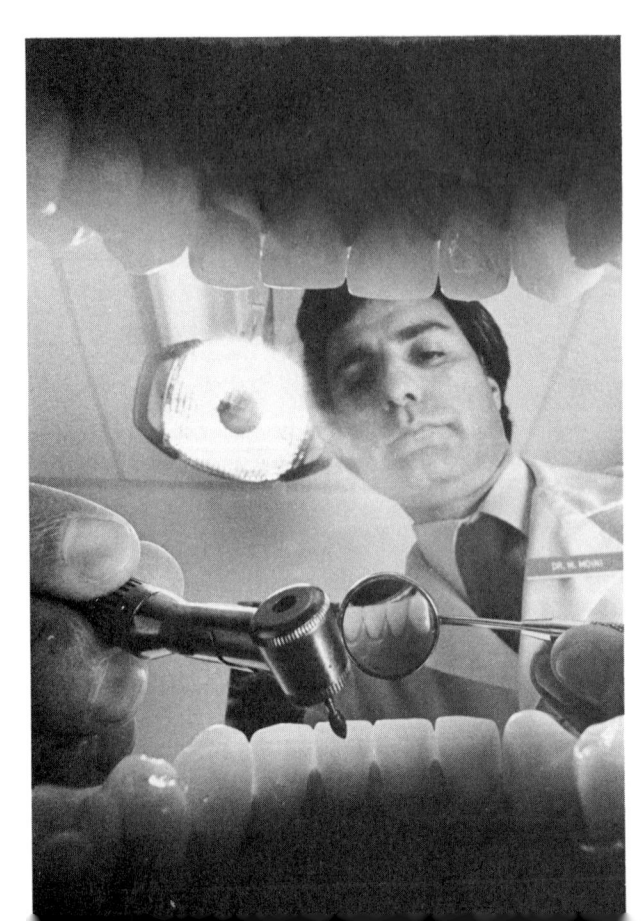

Dentists typically spend 40% of their day filling cavities and applying sealants that protect patients' teeth. The balance of their time is given to preparing prosthetics and doing root canal and gum work.

also have the manual dexterity to fit bridges or dentures into the patient's mouth in a way that ensures his or her comfort.

There are dental specialties dealing with several of these areas, but a typical general dentist, especially a younger one trained in the most up-to-date methods, performs root canal and periodontal work. He or she will send patients to a specialist only when a case is particularly complicated.

Most dental work is done under analgesia or local anesthetic, but many patients come to the dentist dreading pain. Their fear adds stress to the dentist's job. At the same time that he performs delicate, painstaking work he must also relax and soothe the patient.

The American Dental Association points out that dentistry offers an exceptional career opportunity for women and minorities. In the mid-1980s the ratio of black dentists to the black population was 1 to 7,000, whereas the ratio of dentists to the total U.S. population was 1 to 2,000. At the same time, 25% of first-year dental students were women, but only 2% of practicing dentists were women.

Because dentistry is a field with few emergencies, flexible hours—full- or part-time—are available to someone willing to work in another dentist's office and to share a practice. Ninety percent of active dentists are in private practice, and of those 75% practice alone and 17% share office space with only one other practitioner. Many dentists enter private practice by buying the practice—office, equipment, and patient list—of a dentist who is retiring.

The shrinking number of dental students has caused observers to project a supply of dentists that will match the demand for dental services in the future. Forecasters admit, however, that successful anticavity measures for children may cut into the overall need for dental services.

Education

Most dentists have a college degree, but it is possible to enter some dental schools after only two years of undergraduate work. To be admitted to dental school a student must demonstrate above-average scholastic ability and some degree of manual dexterity.

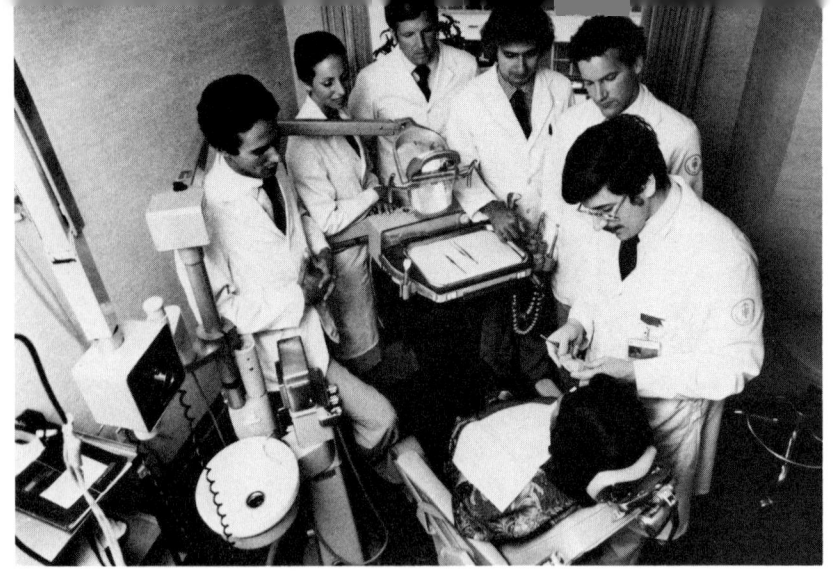

As primary-care physicians, dentists often detect the first signs of serious disease in their patients. Here, dental students look on as a practitioner examines the teeth of a cancer patient.

Dental school is usually a four-year course, though there are a few three-year programs and Harvard University's program lasts five. Programs are usually divided into three broad areas: basic health sciences, such as anatomy and physiology, with an emphasis on dental aspects; application of those health sciences in the dental area, including diagnosis, treatment planning, and treatment; and practice management, which features such topics as patient psychology, the use of aides, business management, professional ethics, and community health. Dental specialists, such as orthodontists and endodontists, continue their schooling for an additional two or three years.

Like aspiring doctors, students considering dentistry should include basic science courses in their high school and college programs. During the 1980s there was a sharp drop in applicants to dental school, from 15,734 in 1975–76 to 6,499 in 1984–85. As a result, the percentage of applicants accepted for enrollment has increased from 37% to 78%.

Average dental school tuition ranges from a low of $2,000 to $8,000 per year for residents of state schools to $6,000 to $12,000 per year at private schools and for out-of-state residents at state schools. Dental students also must pay roughly $6,000 in instrument costs over their four years in school, in addition to paying for books, room, and board.

In 1984, the average dental student graduated from school $32,000 in debt. According to the American Dental Association

(ADA), most dental students cover direct educational (tuition) expenses through loans they manage to pay off within ten years after they have established a practice.

DENTAL SPECIALTIES

More than 80% of dental school graduates become general practitioners who offer a wide variety of care. Those who go on for two or three years of additional training may enter the following specialty fields.

Pedodontia: A pedodontist specializes in the care of children's teeth through adolescence and may also treat handicapped people of all ages.

Orthodontia: Orthodontists prescribe and fit braces to straighten crooked or badly spaced teeth and to correct the bite and alignment of the jaws. Orthodontia is used, for the most part, to treat teenagers, though some younger children and adults are also now wearing braces. Nearly 60% of dental specialists are either orthodontists or dental surgeons.

Endodontia: An endodontist deals with diseases of the dental pulp and usually with root canal therapy, which involves work on the root canal (the tooth's nerve) and surrounding tissue.

Oral and maxillofacial surgery: Specialists in this area extract teeth and treat injuries, diseases, and deformities of the mouth, jaws, and face, such as cleft lip and palate (a congenital defect that leaves the sufferer with a hole in the roof of the mouth).

Oral pathology: Oral pathologists are laboratory dentists who perform tests to diagnose oral problems.

A dental hygienist takes X rays. Later, the dentist will examine the film for signs of tooth decay. Hygienists also clean teeth and, in some instances, recall patients for periodic examinations.

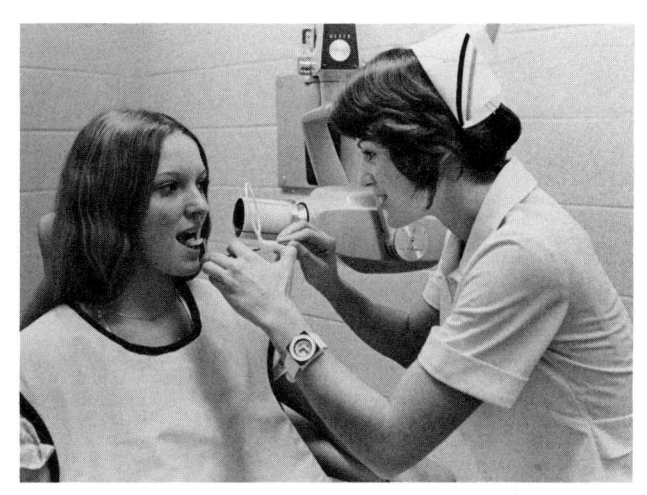

Periodontia: Periodontists treat gum disease, which is common among older people.

Prosthodontitia: Prosthodontists fit and design bridgework and dentures to replace missing teeth and design substitutes for missing oral tissues. They work in laboratories rather than with patients.

Public-health dentists: Dentists in the public-health field promote public awareness throughout the world about measures for preventing and treating dental diseases.

DENTAL HYGIENISTS

Dental hygienists usually work under the supervision of a dentist in a busy private practice office. Hygienists are experts in cleaning teeth and perform a variety of other jobs as well. They take and develop X rays, which are interpreted by the dentist; examine the patient's mouth, noting their findings on a chart; and instruct the patient in good oral hygiene. In certain offices the hygienist may have the responsibility of recalling patients for periodic examinations and may also set his own schedule—or, more likely hers: The typical dental hygienist is a woman who has been working fewer than seven years and makes between $125 and $175 a day.

Like dentists, hygienists must be licensed by the state where they practice. They must also pass a written National Board Examination. To qualify for licensing, a hygienist must have completed two or three years of college in an accredited program. Programs are offered at community colleges, dental schools, technical institutes, and colleges and universities. Undergraduate programs are popular and often have waiting lists of applicants.

It is also possible to receive a bachelor's degree in education, psychology, business, or health administration and then obtain a master's degree in dental hygiene as preparation for licensing.

The courses a dental hygienist studies include basic science, oral anatomy, histology (the study of cells), nutrition, dental materials, first aid, psychology, sociology, public health, and oral pathology (the study of disease). The student hygienist, often working 10 hours a day, also works on patients—some of whom the student herself is expected to provide.

A Day in the Life of a Physical Therapist

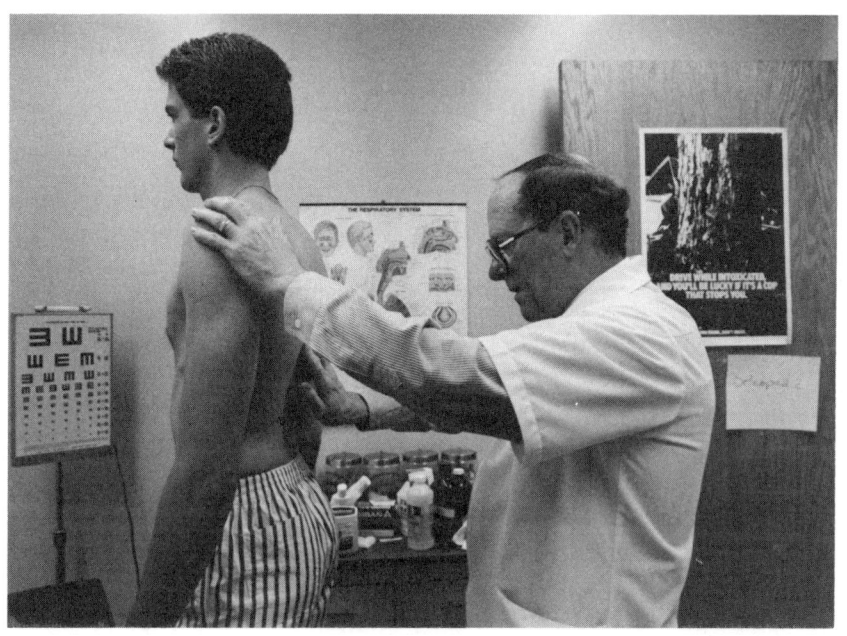

Physical therapist Michael Gavin examines a high school student for signs of scoliosis, a curvature of the spine that, if not treated, can cause severe pain later in life.

It is 8:15 on a Tuesday morning in May at Joseph Foran High School in Milford, Connecticut. Its grounds are leafy and green and dotted with pink dogwood trees. Michael Gavin, a physical therapist, pulls into a parking space in the faculty lot.

Four times a year, Gavin conducts physical examinations at each of Milford's three high schools. Today, Gavin will see to the orthopedic component of the prescreening physicals given to male and female athletes. These physicals are part of a pioneering program developed by the Sports Medicine Institute at Lenox Hill

Hospital in New York City.

The goal of this program is to examine each student athlete for any physical disabilities that may hinder his or her performance or endanger his or her well-being. A prime target of Gavin's examination is scoliosis, a curvature of the spine that, if severe and untreated, can cause pain later in life. If he spots either a C curve or an S curve in the student's upper back, Gavin asks him or her if the condition is being treated and notes the answer on the examination form each student carries. Another concern is excessive tightness or looseness in knee, hip, or ankle joints, which can make an athlete more vulnerable to injury. If he finds these conditions, Gavin may recommend putting braces on the joint to protect it or advise the athlete to perform exercises that will strengthen the joint or make it more flexible.

Gavin asks the athletes if they have any pain. If they do, he tries to locate its cause and, in so doing, draws on his considerable training and skill. Because of the body's *kinetic* (motion) *chain*, a pain in the knee may be caused by a problem in the foot or hip as well as by a direct injury to the knee itself.

Gavin's destination this morning is the nurse's suite of offices, consisting of a waiting room, four examination rooms, and a bathroom, all connected by a long, narrow hall. The waiting-room table is filled with pamphlets with such titles as "Exercise: Design for Life," "Teenage Pregnancy: Everybody's Problem," and "What's a Nice Girl Like Me Doing with a Disease Like This?" Every possible inch of wall space is filled with posters urging the students to practice safe behavior.

Before students reach Gavin's orthopedic station, they visit the school nurse, who checks their height, weight, and blood pressure. They then move on to the orthopedic examination room, a nurse's station with an examining table, a sink, a refrigerator, a few chairs, and a side table containing alcohol, tongue depressors, and Band-Aids. Gavin will spend the next six hours in this room.

Out in the hall about 35 football players—freshmen, sophomores, and juniors—stand around laughing and talking. There is a wide assortment of physical specimens —tall and short, fat and thin, in shape and out of shape. There are weight lifters and beach goers (Milford is situated on Long Island Sound), first-stringers and scrubs. When they enter the examination room the kidding stops and the boys fall quiet.

Gavin begins the first examination. He asks Tim, who is tall and blond, to take off his shirt. Tim lifts his bent arms to shoulder height and stretches out his legs for an inspection of his knee-joint mobility. "What are you going out for?" Gavin asks.

"Football."

"What position?"

"Quarterback."

"Have you played before?"

"I played last year and last summer I went to a camp in Glassboro, New Jersey, for quarterbacks and receivers." He points to the logo on his T-shirt.

As he flexes Tim's feet to test the motion of his ankles, Gavin asks, "Any injuries?"

"None. Quarterback isn't a contact position."

"Right."

Tim stands with his back to Gavin, who runs his fingers along the athlete's spine, tracing a faint C curve. He asks, "Is your physician following this?" Tim replies that his family doctor has been observing his back and has taken some X rays. Gavin notes the mild curvature on Tim's examination form so that it will be brought to the doctor's attention. Tim now admits he had a back problem, that he played before it was healed, and that the condition worsened. Gavin notes this on the form.

After leaving Gavin's "office," each student proceeds to the participating pediatrician for a full physical examination, including a reading of the medical history filled out by their parents.

"Any pain now?" Gavin asks Tim.

"No." Gavin instructs Tim to put his shirt back on. His part of Tim's examination is complete and he calls in the next boy.

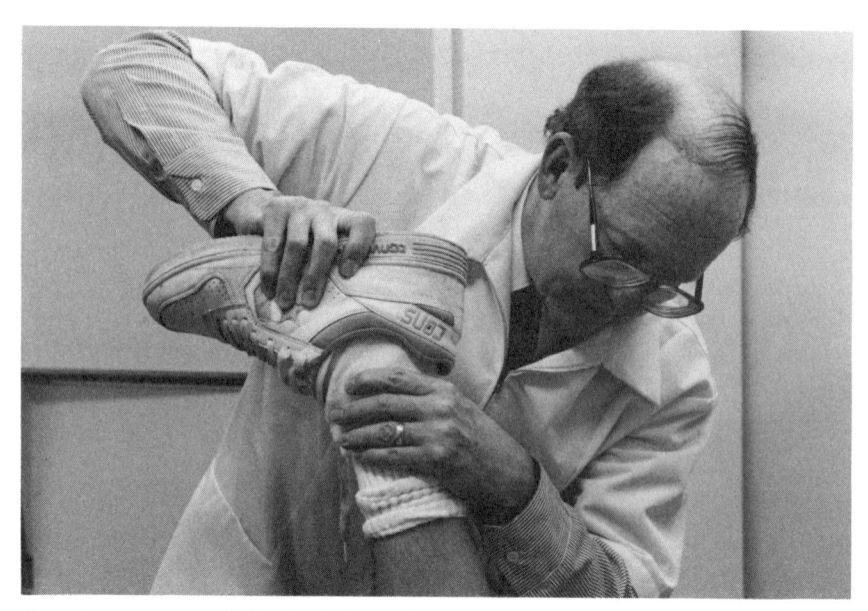

A major concern of physical therapists is excessive tightness or looseness in knee, hip, or ankle joints. Such a condition may require that the patient wear a protective brace.

The biggest health problem in this country is the lack of mandatory physical education. Students should have it three times a week. A national fitness survey has shown that fitness for the American schoolchild is going down while that for adults is going up. We are shamefully neglecting the fitness component of education. It makes me angry to see the boys here who have the desire to play sports but are not in condition to play. That shouldn't be happening in this country.

The examinations continue. Eric, the 11th boy checked by Gavin, has evidently been lifting weights, something Gavin asks all the athletes about. Gavin asks Eric the same questions he asked Tim, but he does not receive the same answers. Eric is not only going out for a guard position on the football team but also runs track in the winter and plays shortstop on the school baseball team. He admits he has sustained a number of injuries and that his knee bothers him regularly. Gavin examines the knee, moving the leg up and down and from side to side and moving the kneecap up and down. None of these motions causes Eric any pain. Gavin moves up and down the leg to the hip and the ankle, rotating and testing for excessive tightness and looseness. He asks Eric to walk forward and backward, first on his heels, then on his toes.

Traditional medicine would look at the injuries of a boy like Eric and recommend that he give up sports. Sports medicine, on the other hand, says there has to be a reason why he is getting injured and that we can correct it so he can keep playing. Eric is a three-letter man. It could turn out that one of his sports would mean a scholarship to college, or at least some financial aid. Even with adults our approach is to substitute one aerobic sport for another when injuries require discontinuing the first sport. When a runner badly injures her knees, our first recommendation is that she take up swimming.

By 10:45 A.M., Gavin has examined the football players and is starting to examine eighth-grade girls who have been bused from their grammar school for today's physicals. Most of the girls expect to compete on the volleyball or swimming teams the following year.

Many have already been active in gymnastics or dance, activities that often result in lordosis, or sway back. Gavin examines the girls for this condition. He finds few injuries. The girls are younger than the boys, with less of a history of participation in sports and virtually none in contact sports such as football.

I am continually asking myself, especially when I am examining boys, 'Is he telling me everything? Is he really pain free?' Many times you don't get the full story because a boy—and, sometimes, a girl too—is afraid that if he tells us something bad he won't be able to participate in sports. I often feel like a detective as I try to smoke out hidden injuries."

At 2:30 P.M., the examinations end, and Gavin stops briefly at his home near Long Island Sound. He eats a lunch of yogurt, bananas, and strawberries. By 3:30 he is in his office at the Physical Therapy/Human Performance Center. There, working with four other physical therapists, Gavin sees patients who are recovering from surgery, who have incurred fractures, been in car accidents, or suffer from lower back pain. The staff also treats workers injured on the job and victims of stroke, severe arthritis, and multiple sclerosis.

Usually several people undergo treatments at any given time, each in a different room. Some patients exercise and others use moist heat, ultrasound, or whirlpool baths to relax muscles, reduce spasms, and prepare the injured area for exercise. This May afternoon there is one patient on a stationary bicycle and another on the exercise table. On other occasions, Gavin may have a patient in either cervical (neck) or pelvic (hip) traction (traction is a way to

85

put a limb, bone, or group of muscles under tension, usually by means of weights and pulleys that keep broken bones rigid or that overcome muscle spasms.)

Gavin's work ends at 6:30 P.M. Some days, however, he stops by Milford General Hospital, where he has a practice that includes helping postoperative patients return to normal functioning. Some are adjusting to crutches or to other devices or to his pioneering two-temperature pool therapy program. Gavin devised this program to aid people with acute back problems, neurological problems such as multiple sclerosis, and spasms. Hot water helps their ailments; cool water allows them to pursue an aerobic training program. In this unique program, Gavin puts patients through a three-step regimen. They begin by exercising faceup, progress to using SCUBA (Self-Contained Underwater Breathing Apparatus) equipment in facedown exercises, and finish with a procedure that calls for them to stand vertically in deep water.

Gavin started practicing physical therapy in 1962—after receiving a bachelor of science degree and then completing a 14-month course at Columbia University's College of Physicians and Surgeons. He has continued to study and is one course short of the requirements for a master's degree in physical therapy. The American Physical Therapy Association, the field's professional organization, is divided into many different specialty sections. Gavin belongs to the orthopedic, sports medicine, cardiopulmonary, obstetrics and gynecology (he does prenatal exercise with pregnant women in his 83-degree pool), and private practice sections. There are also sections in dealing with children, the elderly, and other groups.

One of the best things about being a physical therapist is the variety of work available. You can work in a hospital, an office, a school system. You can make house calls with visiting nurses. Also, they are doing a tremendous amount of research and we are really learning how to make people function better. We're learning prevention as well as cure. It's an exciting field."

• • • •

CHAPTER 8

ALLIED HEALTH CAREERS

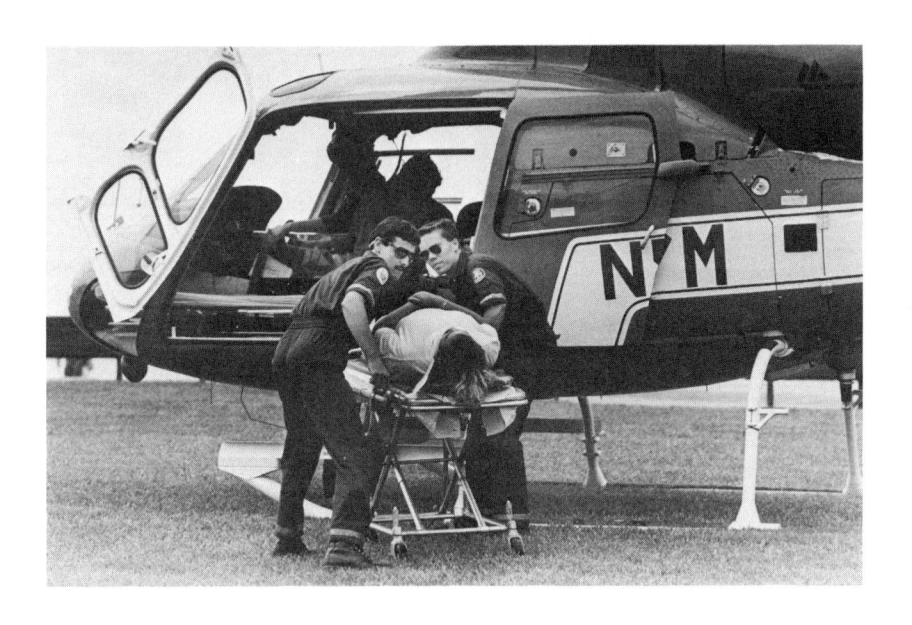

Aside from those of physician, nurse, and dentist, there are more than 100 jobs in the health-care field. According to the AMA, these allied health jobs are filled by "health-related personnel who fulfill necessary functions in the health-care system, including assisting, facilitating, and complementing the work of physicians and other health-care specialists."

The number of allied health careers has grown markedly in recent decades, for two reasons. First, rapid advances in medical technology have created a need for professionals adept at using new and complex instruments. Second, health-care experts have determined that the most effective patient care is provided by a team of professionals working closely together. Allied health careers include emergency medical technicians and pharmacists. Their responsibilities range from the emotional counseling provided by social workers to the record keeping of medical assistants.

The following list of careers mentions some of the many options available in allied health work. These jobs have been divided into "lab" and "people" specialties, although some careers cross into both.

Careers Working with People

Physician Assistant: Physician assistants work under the supervision of physicians, usually internists, surgeons, and pediatricians. Their workplace may be in an office, hospital, or clinic, and their duties vary according to their education, experience, state laws, and the practices of the doctor who employs them. Physician assistants often take patient histories, perform routine physical examinations and electrocardiograms, draw blood for testing, and analyze urine. They may also give injections, make incisions, and put casts on limbs. In some states they are allowed to prescribe medication. Physician assistants hired by hospitals advise patients about physical and mental health, diet, and various types of therapy.

Most physician assistant programs require two years of college followed by a two-year program equally split between classroom and laboratory science study and supervised work with patients. Physician assistants are paid more than most other people in allied health careers.

Emergency Medical Technician: Emergency medical technicians, or EMTs, provide emergency care under the direction of a physician—often by radio communication—for acutely ill or injured patients before they reach the hospital. They work in hospital and private ambulances, in emergency rooms, and for police, fire, and other public-service departments.

The training, work, and certification of EMTs was greatly standardized by the Highway Safety Act of 1966 and in 1970, when the National Registry of Emergency Medical Technicians was established. The Registry recognizes four different job titles:

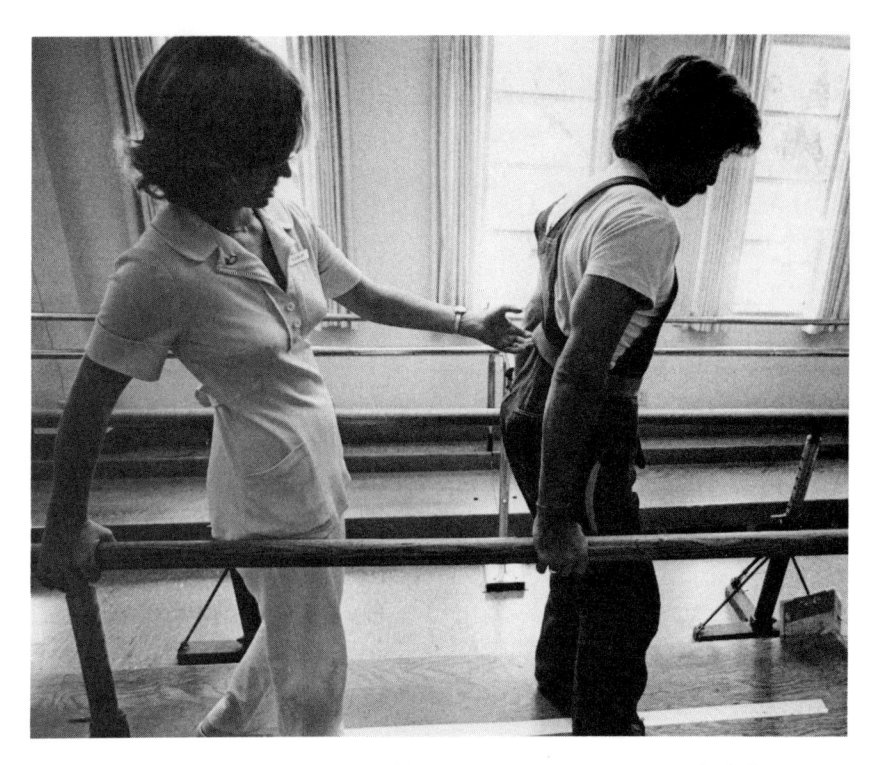

A physical therapist helps a disabled patient exercise at a rehabilitation center. Treatments using heat, cold, or electricity can also improve a patient's mobility.

EMT non-ambulance, who work as a surgical tech, lab tech, X-ray tech, orderly, RN, LPN, and a military corpsman who has not had field service; EMT-ambulance; EMT-intermediate; and EMT-paramedic.

The first two classifications receive the same training, a 100-hour practical and didactic (classroom) program. It includes instruction in CPR (cardiopulmonary resuscitation), how to relieve an airway obstruction, bleeding and shock, fractures, body injuries, emergency childbirth, removal of trapped victims, the legal aspects of prehospital care, vehicle operation and maintenance, and communication and documentation.

The EMT-intermediate training adds instruction in patient assessment, managing shock, using intravenous tubes, and keeping the patient's airways open.

EMT-paramedic training, which can begin upon completion of the first EMT course, takes from 600 to 1,000 hours. During this time, the EMT refines his or her knowledge of life-support

CAREERS IN HEALTH CARE

skills, goes on to study heart monitoring and advanced airway maintenance (using respirators and other sophisticated equipment), and learns how to administer medication. EMT-paramedics are also trained to deal with psychological crises.

Physical Therapist: Physical therapists and their assistants work with people physically disabled as a result of accident, illness, or handicap. In most states, patients must be referred to a therapist by a physician. However, as of 1989, 14 states granted therapists more independence.

Physical therapists work in hospitals, nursing homes, schools for handicapped children, rehabilitation centers, private offices, and in college and university programs as athletic trainers and teachers.

Before prescribing a program, physical therapists evaluate a patient's joint motion, strength, muscle endurance, stability when walking, and ability to perform activities required in daily living. Treatments include exercise and the use of heat, cold, or electricity to relieve pain or to improve a patient's mobility.

Physical therapists complete a four-year program, unless they have a college degree. In that case they must pass a one- or two-year course that leads to a certificate or a master's degree. Therapy assistants complete a two-year associate degree program.

A technician operates an electroencephalograph (EEG), an instrument that detects and records brain waves. Innovations in medical technology have widened opportunities in health care.

Allied Health Careers

Occupational Therapist: "Occupational therapist" is a slight misnomer. "Activity therapist" is more accurate. For although helping handicapped and disabled people find useful jobs is an important part of these specialists' work, they also often assist the emotionally troubled or the extremely elderly who are in need not so much of jobs as of independence, self-reliance, and meaningful activities. An occupational therapist may help a patient to shop, to cook, to master equipment designed to compensate for disability, and to modify work and living space for the purpose of easing the patient's daily life.

Occupational therapists work in hospitals, schools, and mental- and community-health agencies. Their training consists of a special four-year bachelor's degree program including course work in science and psychology and at least six months of supervised work experience. College graduates can enroll in programs that offer certificates and a master's degree in social work. According to the National Association of Social Workers, social work is "a profession devoted to helping people function as well as they can within their environment. Its practitioners do so by providing counseling and services to clients as well as by working for improved social conditions." They often achieve this goal by lobbying to change legislation and social policy.

Speech-Language Pathologists and Audiologists: Speech-language pathologists and audiologists are specialists in talking and hearing problems. Speech-language pathologists work with people who have speech and language disabilities; audiologists focus on hearing problems. Some specialists, however, work in both areas.

Pathologists and audiologists often aid children who have not begun to speak at the expected age or who suffer from speech defects, such as a lisp. They also assist older people who must learn again to speak as the result of a stroke. Speech-language pathologists and audiologists use advanced equipment to test for hearing impairments. They must also be sensitive and patient—many of the children and adults they work with feel humiliated and frustrated by their inability to communicate. Many speech-language pathologists and audiologists work in hospitals. Some also set up private practices that allow them to arrange flexible hours.

This career requires both a bachelor's degree and a master's degree in speech and language pathology or audiology.

CAREERS IN HEALTH CARE

Respiratory Therapy Technician: The task of the respiratory therapy technician is to improve a patient's breathing. Under the joint supervision of a respiratory therapist and a physician, the technician uses many different methods and machines that help him or her make sure the patient's airways are open and that body tissue is receiving sufficient oxygen. The technician may have to explain the goals of respiratory therapy to the patient, instruct the patient in self-help equipment, perform cardiopulmonary resuscitation in an emergency, and maintain records that describe treatment and the patient's response to it. A one-year program, along with a high-school degree or equivalent, provides the required education and training.

Perfusionist: The perfusionist operates special equipment that regulates the patient's blood circulation or breathing during surgery. The need often arises during open heart surgery such as a cardiopulmonary (heart/lung) bypass operation, when surgeons replace clogged arteries with open ones. The perfusionist is expert at extracorporeal (outside the body) circulation and helps the physician select the appropriate equipment and techniques.

Perfusionists work for hospitals or medical service groups such as HMOs. This is a new field and one in which demand often exceeds supply, making it one of the higher paid allied health

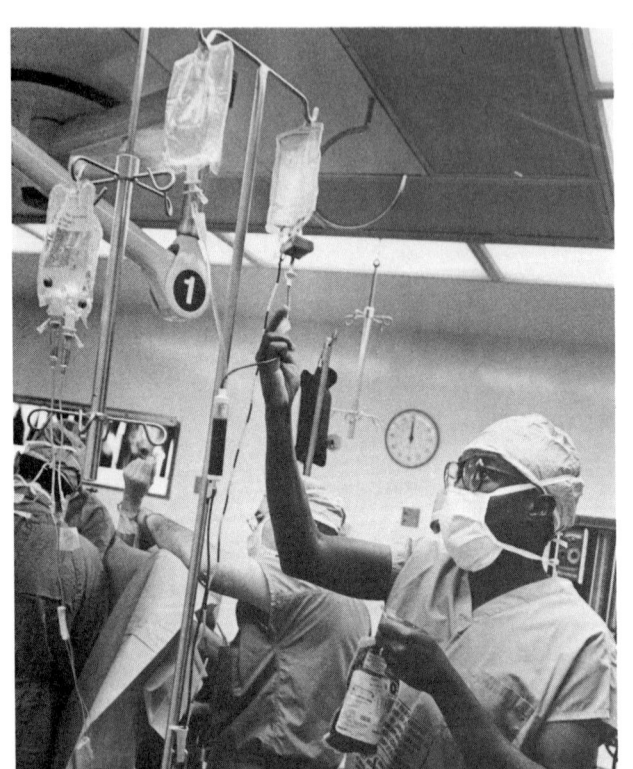

A perfusionist operates equipment that regulates a patient's blood circulation during surgery. Like most perfusionists, this man works in a hospital operating room.

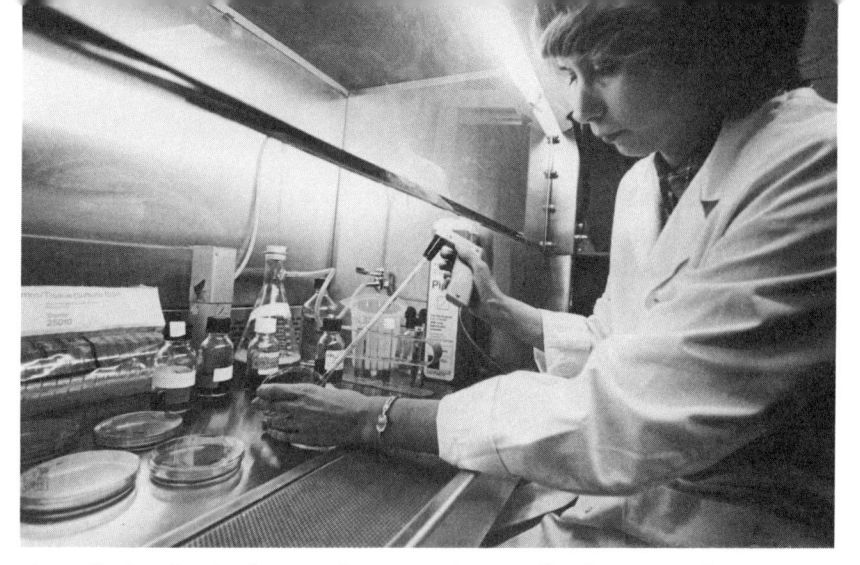

A medical technologist examines a patient's cell cultures in a hospital laboratory. Her findings will be passed on to a pathologist or other scientist who will then determine what treatment the patient needs.

careers that do not require a college degree. The training program lasts one to two years. The prerequisite is a background in medical technology, respiratory therapy, or nursing.

Careers in Laboratories

Medical Technologist: Medical technologists perform sophisticated diagnostic laboratory tests on tissues, blood, and other body fluids using highly precise instruments. Medical technologists work with pathologists and other scientists and may supervise medical technicians who perform routine, uncomplicated procedures that are easy to interpret and correct. Most medical technologists work in hospital laboratories, but some work in physicians' offices, the armed forces, and pharmaceutical or other industrial companies.

Training for this job calls for 90 college-semester hours that include several science courses and one year of professional/clinical education in an accredited medical technology program. As the health-care industry becomes more cost conscious, however, opportunities in this area may dwindle.

Bioanalyst: Bioanalysts are laboratory scientists who direct and sometimes supervise clinical laboratories. Their schooling in scientific disciplines, such as chemistry and biology, sets them apart from many other clinical laboratory scientists. Bioanalysts must also be skilled administrators. They hold a bachelor's degree in medical technology, specialize in biochemistry, and ultimately attain a master's or, preferably, a doctorate degree.

Biomedical Engineer: Biomedical engineers solve biological and medical problems by applying engineering methods to design equipment such as dialysis machines or heart pacemakers, which help stabilize the heart's rhythm.

Biomedical engineers may also design instruments that measure the body's activities. One such instrument, the electrocardiograph machine, monitors heart action. Biomedical engineers must have at least a bachelor's degree in engineering, physics, or a biological science. Many biomedical engineers also have graduate degrees in biomedical engineering or a related applied engineering science.

Dietitian: Dietitians promote and maintain health, prevent or treat illness, and aid rehabilitation by prescribing a proper diet for patients and showing them how to select appropriate foods and adhere to a strict diet. Dietitians often plan meals for hospitals or other institutions, with an eye toward lowering the fat and salt content. Some advise individual patients. Dietitians must complete a four-year bachelor's degree in dietetics, nutrition, or home economics and gain firsthand experience in the field.

Dietitians are commonly aided by dietetic technicians, who complete a two-year associate degree program. Dietetic assistants, who study for one year after high school, assist dietitians by supervising food production or helping hospital patients choose their food for the day.

Medical Illustrator: A medical illustrator is an artist who is qualified by academic knowledge and clinical experience to communicate medical and biological information through books, movies, television, computer graphics, three-dimensional exhibits, and prostheses (artificial limbs). Illustrators serve a variety of functions, ranging from education to advertising.

High school students interested in medical illustration should take as many science and art courses as possible. In colleges, medical illustrators usually major in art; some, however, major in zoology or combine majors in art and biology. The Association of Medical Illustrators has given accreditation to five postgraduate programs. They last from two to three years and balance science courses, such as neuroanatomy, gross anatomy, and histology (the science dealing with the microscopic identification of tissues and cells), with art courses, such as illustration techniques for publication and exhibit design and construction.

CHAPTER 9

ACCEPTING THE CHALLENGE

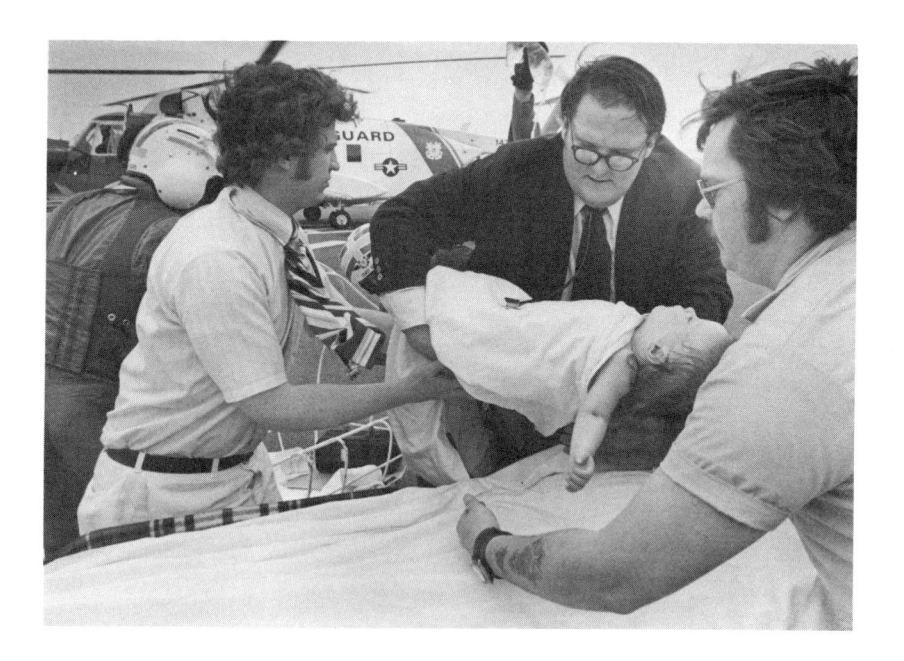

Health care offers a huge diversity of careers—ranging from the traditional settings of a hospital or private practice to the exotic overseas posts available through the Peace Corps or the World Health Organization, an agency of the United Nations. The government also supplies many health-care professionals with jobs, either as part of the Veteran's Administration, the largest health-care system in the United States, in federal agencies such as the Public Health Service, or in the armed forces.

No matter where a career in health care may take you, and no matter what particular career you choose, it is important to keep in mind that a health career often means frustration, fatigue, even depression. At the same time, however, careers in health care offer many advantages lacking in more traditional nine-to-five jobs. For each frustration there is a small triumph, for each patient lost there are many lives saved or improved.

As one young gastroenterologist put it, working in health care reminds her that medical knowledge, when translated into the means to save a life, can be a very real example of human power. She considers herself to be searching "for the pieces of a puzzle that don't fit perfectly and then working to restore the balance, whether it's in an individual or a larger situation. In the individual you are looking at a one-time application of medical knowledge. However, to make a good choice you must understand all the possible ways to treat the disease in order to make that choice. The thing that makes medicine so wonderful is the concept that there is something powerful and absolutely wonderful about life and that is what medicine is all about. What we are doing is restoring life or making a life more meaningful, or making the quality of life better, and fitting all the science into this power is truly exciting."

This power touches every career in health care. The field not only allows you to satisfy your intellectual curiosity but also enables you serve the public good. In health care, you can be instrumental in saving lives in a Third World country in a distant corner of the map or at a highway accident a block away from your home. In either place, the health-care worker must accept the challenge of professionalism. This often means accepting that there is yet no cure for a particular disease and that some patients will certainly die. At the same time, you will also know that your concern and skill has made life better for people in your care.

Whatever branch of health care you decide to enter, you will be responsible, in some way, for another person's well-being and, at times, will greatly influence his or her future.

Not every person is suited to a career in health care—you must decide for yourself whether you are equal to the challenge.

• • • •

APPENDIX: FOR MORE INFORMATION

A compendium of all the health-care organizations in the United States would fill a book. Someone interested in information about a particular field should contact a local medical college. An administrator there can provide a general overview of many health-care professions and may have the names of doctors, nurses, and other health-care professionals willing to explain their particular field.

Another resource is a nearby hospital. Its administrator can furnish the names and addresses of health-care programs. For instance, in the Oklahoma City vicinity, Luanne Kallas-Burton of career placement at the University of Oklahoma's School of Public Health (405-271-2232) can provide appropriate information for those interested in the various paths to a health-care career. Quebec residents who want to learn about medical education or postgraduate specialties should call the number for general information for the McGill University Faculty of Medicine at 514-398-3515; someone there will direct the caller to the appropriate university departments.

A useful guidebook to health-care associations throughout the nation is the *Encyclopedia of Associations* (Detroit: Gale Research Company, 1987). It lists the names, addresses, and phone numbers of organizations that deal with the entire range of health-care professions. For information on nursing in North Carolina, for example, one would contact the National Federation of Licensed Practical Nurses at 214 S. Driver Street, Durham, NC, 27703 (919-596-9609). Midwesterners interested in osteopathy, on the other hand, might write or call the American Osteopathic Association at 212 E. Ohio Street, Chicago, IL, 60611 (312-280-5800). This volume also provides a summary of the publications and information available through each organization.

For those to whom neither this encyclopedia nor a medical education institution are easily accessible, the following general umbrella organizations may act as starting points in researching health careers.

CAREERS IN HEALTH CARE

American Dental Association (ADA)
211 E. Chicago Ave.
Chicago, IL 60611
(312) 440-2500

American Foundation for
  Alternative Health Care,
  Research and Development
25 Landfield Ave.
Monticello, NY 12701
(914) 794-8181

American Medical
  Association (AMA)
535 N. Dearborn St.
Chicago, IL 60610
(312) 645-5000

American Nurses' Association
2420 Pershing Rd.
Kansas City, MO 64105
(816) 474-5720

FURTHER READING

Allied Health Education Directory. 16th ed. Chicago: American Medical Association, 1978.

Bluestone, Naomi, M.D. *So You Want To Be a Doctor?: The Realities of Pursuing Medicine as a Career.* New York: Lothrop, Lee & Shepard, 1981.

Cohen, Richard L. *House Officer: Becoming a Medical Specialist.* New York: Plenum, 1988.

Frederickson, Keville. *Opportunities in Nursing Careers.* Lincolnwood, IL: National Textbook, 1983.

Heron, Jackie, R.N. *Exploring Careers in Nursing.* New York: The Rosen Publishing Group, 1986.

Keyes, Fenton. *The Allied Health Field.* New York: Richard Rosens Press, 1978.

———. *Your Future in a Paramedic Career.* New York: Richard Rosens Press, 1979.

Morgan, Elizabeth. *The Making of a Woman Surgeon.* New York: Putnam, 1980.

Nash, David B., M.D. *Future Practice Alternatives in Medicine.* New York: Igaku-Shoin, 1987.

Nassif, Janet Zhun. *Handbook of Health Careers.* New York: Human Sciences Press, 1980.

Nuland, Sherwin B. *Doctors: The Biography of Medicine.* New York: Knopf, 1988.

Seide, Diane. *Careers in Health Services.* New York: Dutton, 1982.

Smith, David B., and Barbara Zimmerman. *Careers in Health Care: The Professionals Give You the Inside Picture About Their Jobs.* Boston: Beacon, 1979.

Swanson, Barbara. *Careers in Health Care.* Homewood, IL: Dow Jones Irwin, 1984.

Viscott, David S., M.D. *The Making of a Psychiatrist.* New York: Arbor House, 1972.

GLOSSARY

abortion pregnancy termination through removal of a fetus

adolescence stage of human psychological, physiological, and psychosexual growth usually defined as occurring between the ages of 13 and 22

allograft surgery whereby diseased tissue, organs, or bone is replaced with healthy matter from either a living donor or a cadaver

anesthesiologist physician who uses a variety of drugs and gases to lessen patients' discomfort during surgery, using either a local anesthetic to numb a concentrated area or a general anesthetic to induce a complete state of unconsciousness

arteriosclerosis hardening of the arteries

arthroscopic surgery outpatient surgery using small instruments and incisions; performed primarily on athletes

biopsy removal of tissue for examination to help determine whether surgery should be performed

bunions abnormal swellings of the joint at the base of the big toe

cardiologist physician who treats diseases of the heart and of the vessels that carry blood to and from the heart

chiropractor health-care professional who practices under the belief that certain illnesses are due to inhibited nerve function caused by bone misalignment and that human well-being depends on the relationship between structure and function in the human body; although they cannot prescribe drugs or perform surgery, chiropractors often recommend vitamins

dermatologist physician who treats diseases of the skin, hair, and nails

diabetes a disorder caused by the failure of the pancreas to release enough insulin into the bloodstream

CAREERS IN HEALTH CARE

diagnosis-related groups (DRGs) coding system used by health insurance companies to specify which procedures they will cover

electrocardiogram machine that detects abnormal electric impulses in the heart

endocrinologist physician who treats disorders of the hormone system

gastroenterologist physician who treats diseases of the digestive system

geriatrics area of health care focusing on diseases and psychology of the elderly

gerontology study of aging and the diseases of the elderly

gynecologist physician who treats disorders of the female reproductive system

health maintenance organizations (HMOs) groups of health-care consumers served by physicians, physician groups, and hospitals—all under contract to provide the full gamut of health-care services

hematology the study of blood

holistic medicine health-care practice involving study of the whole person, taking into account physical, mental, emotional, spiritual, and environmental aspects of the patient's life; this area of health care includes humanistic, psychosomatic, and behavioral medicine and places as much emphasis on education for wellness as on treatment for illness; often involves homeopathic remedies and unorthodox therapies instead of surgery and conventional medicine

infertility a physical inability to produce offspring; in women an inability to conceive; in men an inability to fertilize eggs

internal medicine area of health care specializing in nonsurgical treatment of the internal organs and functions of the body

kidney stones mineral build-ups that block the kidney and thus impede urine flow

laser surgery high-precision surgery using Light Amplification by Stimulated Emission of Radiation; the concentrated beam of pure light produced destroys cells; because of its detailed accuracy, this method is particularly successful in eye surgery

magnetic resonance imaging (MRI) division of radiology that uses magnetized protons and radio-frequency pulses to create images in several layers of the body, enabling trained radiologists to discover diseased internal tissue

Glossary

naturopathy a system of treating disease encouraging the use of natural foods, light, warmth, massage, regular exercise, and the avoidance of drugs

neonatal nursing area of nursing that deals specifically with the infant and mother from birth until six weeks thereafter

nephrology the study of the kidneys

neurologist physician who treats disorders of the nervous system

nurse midwife independent nurse practitioner who cares for essentially healthy women and newborns before, during, and after delivery

obstetrician physician who delivers babies and treats pregnant women

occupational medicine practice that focuses on the health of workers, usually by caring for employees of particular companies

oncologist physician specializing in the treatment of cancer

ophthalmologist physician specializing in the treatment of eye diseases and disorders

orthopedic surgeon physician specializing in treatment of problems affecting muscles and bones

otolaryngology the study of ear, nose, and throat

pathology the study of disease

pediatrician physician who deals with the particular illnesses and medical needs of children

pharmacology the study of drugs

physiotherapist physician who aids the physical rehabilitation of athletes recovering from injuries or illnesses affecting the nerves, muscles, or bones

podiatrist health professional who treats foot diseases and disorders

primary-care physician doctor whom a patient visits before consulting a specialist, to determine the cause of an ailment; includes internal medicine, family, and pediatric practitioners

psychiatrist physician who seeks physical causes of mental problems

radiologist physician who uses X rays and other radioactive substances to produce images of the internal body and/or to destroy diseased cells

residency two- or three-year post–medical school training period in a hospital

rheumatology the study of connective tissues

sonarography method of producing images of the internal body on a screen by using ultrasound to penetrate the body; frequently performed on pregnant women

INDEX

Acupuncturists, 60
Adolescent medicine, 32, 36–37
Alcohol, Drug Abuse, and Mental Health Administration (ADAMHA), 56
Allergy and immunology, 32
Allied health care, 15, 18, 20, 87–94
American Nurses' Association, 63, 65
Anesthesiologists, 14, 51, 69, 70
Anesthetists, nurse. *See* Nurse anesthetists
Audiologists, 91

Bioanalysts, 93
Biomedical engineers, 94
Blue Cross, 19
Blue Shield, 19

Cardiologists, 18, 60
Cardiology, 32, 35, 53–54
Careers, health care
　challenge of, 95–96
　deciding on, 13–16, 22
　education for. *See* Education
Centers for Disease Control (CDC), 56
Chiropractic medicine, 58–59, 60
Community health, 14, 33, 62
Counselors, psychological, 60

Dental hygienists, 80
Dentistry, 15
　primary-care, 75–79
　public-health, 80
Dentists, 72, 87
Dermatology, 44–45

Diagnostic-related groups (DRGs), 19–20
Diagnostic medical sonographers, 50
Dietitians, 94

Education, 15
　for audiologists, 91
　for bioanalysts, 93
　for biomedical engineers, 94
　for chiropractors, 58–59
　for dental hygienists, 80
　for dentists, 77–79
　for dietitians, 94
　for emergency medical technicians, 89–90
　for licensed practical nurses, 73–74
　loans for, 22, 24, 79
　for medical illustrators, 94
　for medical technologists, 93
　for nurse anesthetists, 70
　for occupational therapists, 91
　for perfusionists, 93
　for physical therapists, 90
　for physicians, 23–30
　for public health workers, 56
　for registered nurses, 61, 62–65
　for respiratory therapy technicians, 92
　for speech-language pathologists, 91
Emergency medical technicians, 88–90
Emergency medicine, 33
Endocrinology, 32
Endodontia, 78, 79

104

Index

Exercise physiologists, 60

Family medicine, 33–34, 58
Family practitioners, 20, 52
Federation Licensing Exam (FLEX), 29
Food and Drug Administration (FDA), 56

Gastroenterology, 32
Geriatrics, 20, 32, 33, 37–38
Gerontology. *See* Geriatrics
Gynecology. *See* Obstetrics and gynecology

Health care, changes in, 17–22
Health maintenance organizations (HMOs), 20–22, 34, 40, 92
Hematology, 32
HMOs. *See* Health maintenance organizations (HMOs)
Holistic medicine, 59–60
Home health aides, 74

Infectious diseases, 32
Insurance
  malpractice, 22, 35
  medical, 18, 19–20, 20, 21
Internal medicine, 25, 32–33, 38, 58
Internists, 20, 37, 52

Joint Commission on Accreditation of Health Care Organizations, 29

Laboratories, 93–94
Laboratory technicians. *See* Medical technologists
Lasers, 41
Licensed practical nurses (LPNs). *See* Nurses, licensed practical
Licensing
  for chiropractors, 58
  for dental hygienists, 80
  for holistic medicine practitioners, 60
  for nurses, 65
  for physicians, 27–29

Massage therapists, 60
Medicaid, 19
Medical assistants, 88
Medical College Admissions Test (MCAT), 24
Medical illustrators, 94
Medical school, 24
  admissions test for, 24
  cost of, 24
  curriculum changes in, 24–25
  women in, 18
Medical technologists, 14, 15, 93
Medical technology, 93
Medicare, 19, 20
Men, in military nursing, 71
Mental health, 48–49
Microsurgery, 41, 46
Midwives. *See* Nurse-midwives
Minorities, in dentistry, 77

National Board of Medical Examiners (NBME), 28
National Institutes of Health (NIH), 56
National Registry of Emergency Medical Technicians, 88–89
National Resident Matching Program, 27
Naturopaths, 60
Neonatologists, 35
Nephrology, 32, 45
Neurology, 52–53
Neurosurgery, 40
Nurse anesthetists, 14, 69–70
Nurse-midwives, 15, 65
Nurses, 15, 18, 20, 51, 87
  child psychiatric, 62
  circulating, 69
  community, 72
  critical-care, 62
  emergency, 68
  licensed practical, 63, 72–74
  military, 71–72
  neonatal, 65, 66–67, 68
  operating room, 68–69
  pediatric, 70–71
  psychiatric, 62
  public-health, 62, 72

105

registered, 61–65, 68–72
school, 15, 71
scrub, 14, 69
visiting, 86
vocational, 63
Nurse's aides, 74
Nursing, 15, 61–74, 93
 alternative careers in, 72–74
Nursing shortage, 63
Nutritionists, 18, 60

Obstetrics and gynecology, 20, 25, 32, 33, 35–36, 44, 86
Occupational medicine, 57–58
Occupational Safety and Health Act, 57
Occupational therapists, 91
Oncology, 18, 32, 35
Ophthalmology, 33, 41–42, 44
Oral pathology, 79
Orderlies, 74
Orthodontia, 78, 79
Orthopedics, 33, 86. See also Surgery, orthopedic
Otolaryngology, 33

Paramedics. See Emergency medical technicians
Pathologists, 93
Peace Corps, 95
Pediatricians, 15, 20, 37, 71, 83
Pediatrics, 20, 25, 32, 33, 34–35, 70–71, 74
Pedodontia, 79
Perfusionists, 15, 92–93
Periodontia, 80
Pharmacology, 53, 55, 74
Pharmacy, 88
Physical education, 83
Physical therapists, 81–86, 90
Physical therapy, 43, 52, 59
Physical therapy assistants, 90
Physician assistants, 88
Physicians, 20, 23, 47, 52, 57, 65, 71, 72, 87, 88
 competency reviews of, 29–30
 female, 18
 in HMOs, 21, 22

oversupply of, 18
patient interaction with, 26
primary care, 31
Physiotherapists, 52
Podiatry, 43–44
Premedical programs, 24
Prenatal specialists, 35
Primary care
 in dentistry, 75–79
 in medicine, 31–38
Prosthodontia, 80
Psychiatric nurse practitioners, 62
Psychiatry, 25, 33, 48–49, 58
Psychologists, 48
Psychotherapy, 48
Public health, 36, 55–56, 57, 80
Public Health Service, 56, 96

Radiation-therapy technologists, 50, 51
Radiology, 33, 49–51
Research, 14, 53
Residencies
 dermatology, 44
 family medicine, 33
 for fourth-year medical students, 27
 occupational medicine, 58
 orthopedic, 43
 pediatric, 35
 surgical, 40
 urology, 46
Residents, 14, 15, 26, 27
Respiratory therapy, 93
Respiratory therapy technicians, 92
Rheumatology, 32

Salaries
 of dental hygienists, 80
 of nurse anesthetists, 70
 of nurses, 64
 of residents, 27
Social work, 48, 57, 88, 91
Specialties
 dental, 79–80
 medical, 47–60
  alternative, 58–60
  primary-care, 31–38

Index

surgical, 39–46
Speech-language pathologists, 91
Sports medicine, 52, 84, 86
Surgeons, 14, 40, 51, 54, 69, 76
Surgery, 40–41, 59, 69
   anesthesia during, 51
   arthroscopic, 43
   colon and rectal, 40
   dermatologic, 45
   general, 33, 58
   laser, 41
   neurological, 40
   open-heart, 14, 92
   ophthalmologic, 41, 42
   oral and maxillofacial, 79
   orthopedic, 18, 42–43, 52. *See also* Orthopedics
   pediatric, 35
   plastic, 40, 42
   podiatric, 44
   thoracic, 40

Teaching, 14
Therapists, 48–49
   massage, 60
   occupational. *See* Occupational therapists
   physical. *See* Physical therapists
Tuition
   dental school, 78
   licensed practical nurse course, 74
   medical school, 24
Urology, 33, 45–46
U.S. Department of Health and Human Services, 56

Veteran's Administration, 95

Women
   in dentistry, 77
   as physicians, 18
World Health Organization, 95

X-ray technicians, 15

PICTURE CREDITS

American Cancer Society: pp. 33, 76, 93; The Bettmann Archive: p. 39; Laimute Druskis/Taurus Photos: pp. 13, 17, 19, 35, 58, 63, 79, 92; Tom Elliot/Taurus Photos: pp. 61, 89; Spencer Grant/Taurus Photos: pp. 47, 87; Debra P. Hershkowitz: pp. 81, 83, 84; Ellis Herwig/Taurus Photos: pp. 21, 70; Eric Kroll/Taurus Photos: p. 59; Phiz Mezey/Taurus Photos: p. 67; Martin Rotker/Taurus Photos: p. 44; Frank Siteman/Taurus Photos: p. 52; Michael Stuckey/Comstock, Inc.: cover; Russell Thompson/Taurus Photos: p. 64; Taurus Photos: p. 41: Richard Wood/Taurus Photos: pp. 15, 25, 26, 28, 37, 42, 50, 55, 70, 75, 76; Shirley Zeiberg/Taurus Photos: pp. 23, 31, 73, 90

Rachel S. Epstein, a freelance writer, holds an M.B.A. from New York University. Her articles have appeared in the *Wall Street Journal*, the *Washington Post*, *Working Woman*, and *Ms*. She is the author of *Alternative Investments, Careers in the Investment World, Investment Banking*, and *Investments and the Law* for the Chelsea House BASIC INVESTOR'S LIBRARY and coauthor of *Biz Speak: A Dictionary of Business Terms, Slang, and Jargon*.

Dale C. Garell, M.D., is medical director of California Childrens Services, Department of Health Services, County of Los Angeles. He is also clinical professor in the Department of Pediatrics and Family Medicine at the University of Southern California School of Medicine and Visiting associate clinical professor of maternal and child health at the University of Hawaii School of Public Health. From 1963 to 1974, he was medical director of the Division of Adolescent Medicine at Children's Hospital in Los Angeles. Dr. Garell has served as president of the Society for Adolescent Medicine, chairman of the youth committee of the American Academy of Pediatrics, and as a forum member of the White House Conference on Children (1970) and White House Conference on Youth (1971). He has also been a member of the editorial board of the *American Journal of Diseases of Children*.

C. Everett Koop, M.D., Sc.D., is Surgeon General, Deputy Assistant Secretary for Health, and Director of the Office of International Health of the U.S. Public Health Service. A pediatric surgeon with an international reputation, he was previously surgeon-in-chief of Children's Hospital of Philadelphia and professor of pediatric surgery and pediatrics at the University of Pennsylvania. Dr. Koop is the author of more than 175 articles and books on the practice of medicine. He has served as surgery editor of the *Journal of Clinical Pediatrics* and editor-in-chief of the *Journal of Pediatric Surgery*. Dr. Koop has received nine honorary degrees and numerous other awards, including the Denis Brown Gold Medal of the British Association of Paediatric Surgeons, the William E. Ladd Gold Medal of the American Academy of Pediatrics, and the Copernicus Medal of the Surgical Society of Poland. He is a Chevalier of the French Legion of Honor and a member of the Royal College of Surgeons, London.

DATE DUE

DEC 18 1989			
JAN 3			
JAN 17			
JAN 19 1994			
FEB 4 1994			
MAR 3 1994			
FEB 24 1995			
DEC 04 1995			
DE 19 '96			
OCT 1 6 2008			

610.69　　Epstein, Rachel　　c.1
Eps　　　　Careers In Health Care

Ludington High School Library